533.9164
V 862 h

✓ W9-DIB-744
3 5674 03797049 9

CONELY BRANCH LIBRARY
4600 MARTIN
DETROIT, MI 48210
(313) 224-6461

The Restless Sea

HUMAN IMPACT

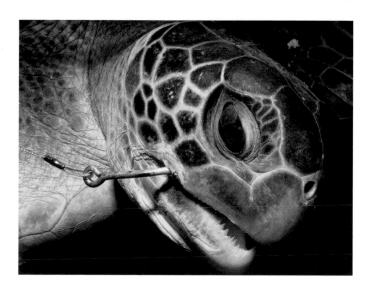

CAROLE GARBUNY VOGEL

Franklin Watts

A Division of Scholastic Inc.
New York • Toronto • London • Auckland • Sydney
Mexico City • New Delhi • Hong Kong
Danbury, Connecticut

APR - - 2004

FOR KARIN MCQUILLAN, with thanks for her listening ear and thoughtful feedback during the writing of the Restless Sea.

Acknowledgments

Many thanks to Professor Peter Guth, Oceanography Department, U.S. Naval Academy, Annapolis, Maryland, who took time from his busy schedule to read and critique the manuscript and answer my many questions. His vast knowledge of the field and keen insight were reflected in his comments.

I am most appreciative of editorial researcher, Kathleen Derzipilski, San Diego, California, for a superb job of fact checking.

I am also grateful to fellow writer Dr. Joyce A. Nettleton for her invaluable criticism, scientific expertise, and sense of humor. Special thanks to students Stephen, Daniel, and Joanna Guth for reading the manuscript from the kid perspective.

Special thanks to my former high school biology teacher, Joan Elger Gottlieb, Ph.D., Pittsburgh, Pennsylvania, for her excellent suggestions.

As usual, I am indebted to the reference librarians at Cary Memorial Library in Lexington, Massachusetts, for their invaluable assistance in tracking down hard to find information.

My sincere appreciation to my husband, Mark A. Vogel, for the encouragement and understanding that have become his hallmark. I would also like to acknowledge the many other people who helped either directly or indirectly.

Finally, my heartfelt thanks to my editor, Kate Nunn, for having faith in my writing ability and the talent to turn my manuscripts into spectacular books.

Photographs © 2003: Corbis Images: 15 top right,16, 17 (AFP), 62 (Theo Allofs), 56 (Australian Picture Library), 29 bottom right (Hal Beral), 15 left (Bettman), 23, 68, 69 (Jonathan Blair), 14 (Gary Braasch), 84 (Rick Doyle), 12 (Natalie Fobes), 58 (Stephen Frink), 42 (Gallo Images), 43 (Raymond Gehman), 34 (Bill Gentile), 49 (Hulton-Deutsch Collection), 48 (Wolfgang Kaehler), 4 (Kit Kittle), 20 (Robert Landau), 82 (Wayne Lawler; Ecoscene), 19 (Larry Lee), 33 (Lester Lefkowitz), 15 bottom right (Joe McDonald), 80, 81 (Charles O'Rear), 51 (Rick Price), 11, 6, 7 (Reuters NewMedia Inc.), 1, 29 center right, 77 center (Jeffrey L. Rotman), 41 (Galen Rowell), 10 (Ron Sanford), 65 (Ed Wargin), 28, 29 left, 29 top right (Douglas P. Wilson/Frank Lane Picture Agency), 36, 37 (Michael S. Yamashita), 72, 73 (Ed Young), 21; Peter Arnold Inc.: 63 (A. Hurtig/UNEP), 74 (W. Min/UNEP); Photo Researchers, NY: 26 (Bill Bachman), 24 (Dan Guravich), 53 (Labat/Jerrican), 76, 77 left (Jeff Rotman); PhotoDisc/Getty Images: cover; Seapics.com: 46 (Clay Bryce), 77 right (Richard Herrmann).

Book design by Marie O'Neill

Vogel, Carole Garbuny.
  Human impact / Carole G. Vogel.
    v. cm. — (The restless sea)
Includes bibliographical references and index.
Contents: Troubled waters — Sea sick — Too many fishermen — The impact of global warming — The human footprint.
  ISBN 0-531-12323-5 (lib. bdg.)   0-531-16680-5 (pbk.)
  1. Marine pollution—Juvenile literature. 2. Nature—Effect of human beings on—Juvenile literature. 3. Global warming—Environmental aspects—Juvenile literature. [1. Marine pollution. 2. Nature—Effect of human beings on. 3. Global warming.] I. Title.
  GC1090.V64 2003
  333.91'64—dc21

                    2003005301

© 2003 Carole Garbuny Vogel
All rights reserved. Published simultaneously in Canada. Printed in the United States of America.
1 2 3 4 5 6 7 8 9 10 R 12 11 10 09 08 07 06 05 04 03

APR - - 2004

CONELY BRANCH

contents

chapter 1

TROUBLED WATERS

If you looked down on Earth from the space shuttle, the ocean would appear blue and still. Instead of three separate bodies of water that we call the Atlantic, Pacific, and Indian Oceans, you would see one huge world ocean that covers nearly three-fourths of the planet's surface. The ocean holds 97 percent of Earth's water and plays a key role in controlling our weather and climate. Billions of years ago, the ocean realm cradled the beginnings of life. Today it provides almost 99 percent of Earth's living space.

Throughout history, humans have taken for granted the bounty of the sea. Teeming with fish and other marine wildlife, the ocean has already fed a multitude of people in the past and it has the potential to feed Earth's rapidly expanding human population in the future. But the ocean means more to human existence than a seemingly unending food supply. More than 70 percent of the oxygen we breathe is generated by marine plants. Healthy coral reefs, wetlands, and barrier islands buffer coastal settlements from frenzied seas and storm-driven floods. Rich deposits of oil and gas in the seafloor help to meet the fuel needs of energy-hungry nations.

Despite our dependence on the sea, the future of the ocean and its wildlife is not clear. Human beings have collectively become one of the most potent forces in nature, transforming the ocean through pollution, overfishing, and uncontrolled coastal development. But we are just one of a bewildering variety of species dependent on the sea, and our actions have caused serious repercussions throughout the marine ecosystem. The ocean is not as resilient as it once seemed. One ominous sign of its ill health is the growing frequency of dead zones.

Shore fishers enjoy a stunning sunset along East Hampton Beach, New York.

DEAD ZONES

Several times during each summer a bizarre scene takes place along the edge of the Gulf of Mexico in Mobile Bay, Alabama. Stressed and dying fish, shrimps, and crabs practically fling themselves onto the beach and into the open ice chests of expectant residents. The locals call these events jubilees. Entire communities come running to celebrate the bounty of the sea, scooping up fish and crustaceans by the bucketful. Although the doomed sea creatures seem to surrender willingly, they have not lost their minds—only their oxygen. They are victims of a local dead zone.

A dead zone forms when the wind and rising tide push oxygen-poor water in the bay toward the shore. Most sea animals cannot survive in oxygen-depleted water. For the hordes of slow-moving and sedentary creatures such as snails, starfish, worms, and anemones, there is no escape. Death comes quickly.

Fast-moving fish, shrimps, and crabs, scramble to safer water or suffocate while trying. However, the fleeing creatures may become trapped between land and sea. Unless they are snatched up by humans or hungry seabirds, some can cling to life waiting until the dead zone

A toxic algae bloom in South Africa's Elands Bay caused an oxygen shortage in the water, forcing a multitude of lobsters from the bay.

7

drifts away. Flounder straddle the ocean's edge, gasping in air and forcing it over their gills. Partially submerged blue crabs blow bubbles out their mouths. Killifish survive on the miniscule amount of oxygen at the very surface of the water. The jubilee ends a few hours later when the tide changes and drives the dead zone out to sea.

Each summer when the winds turn calm, a significantly larger dead zone forms farther offshore in the Gulf of Mexico. Water laden with nitrogen and phosphorus pours into the Gulf from the Mississippi and Atchafalaya river systems. The lighter river water does not mix with the heavier, salty water of the Gulf. Instead it forms a separate layer on top of it, preventing oxygen from the air from reaching the salty water below. Nutrient-rich, the freshwater spurs the massive growth of algae (simple, plantlike organisms) at the surface. When the algae die, they sink to the seafloor, where bacteria feast on them. During a process known as decay, the bacteria eat the dead organisms, breaking down complex molecules into smaller ones. The decay process recycles matter by returning nutrients to the environment. It also consumes nearly all the oxygen in the water, suffocating the inhabitants along the seafloor.

The Gulf's dead zone is no small affair. In some years this underwater death cloud chokes an area roughly the size of New Jersey. The nutrient pollution fueling the dead zone comes mainly from fertilizers spread on fields and from the excrement of farm animals. Most of it originates on farms in the upper Midwest, hundreds of miles upriver. Runoff from cities, towns, and suburbs within the vast Mississippi River basin also contributes. The dead zone disappears each fall when the first hurricane or significant storm stirs up the water and aerates it. Oxygenated water reaches the ocean bottom once again.

Nearly 60 dead zones exist worldwide. One of the worst is in the Baltic Sea, which separates Scandinavia from the rest of northern Europe. This dead zone covers an area nearly the size of Pennsylvania and has caused the virtual extinction of all the bottom-dwelling sea creatures beneath it. On the east coast of the United States, dead zones appear in the Chesapeake Bay, Long Island Sound, and Pamlico Sound.

Nitrogen and phosphorus are found naturally in the ocean. In moderation they are beneficial to ocean food chains because they sustain production of algae without causing colossal algae growth. Algae are the organisms that form the base of most marine food chains.

Nitrogen Fertilizers: A Mixed Blessing

Nitrogen fertilizers rescued Europe from famine. Around 1840 crop yields declined in Europe because of the lack of usable nitrogen in the soil. People began to starve. Guano—seabird droppings high in usable nitrogen—was imported from South America and spread over farmland. Harvests improved significantly. The guano supply seemed limitless—some deposits towered more than 100 feet (30 meters) above the ground. However, by the end of the 1800s it was clear that the guano deposits would soon be exhausted. The race was on to find another solution.

Almost 80 percent of the Earth's atmosphere consists of nitrogen. All living things, including you, need nitrogen to make proteins, the building blocks of cells. Yet most organisms cannot use nitrogen directly. Only nitrogen-fixing bacteria can extract nitrogen from the air and combine it with other elements to form nitrates. The bacteria release nitrates into the soil where plants absorb them through their roots. The nitrates reach you via the food chain.

In 1909 a German chemist named Fritz Haber found a way to mimic these bacteria and he produced nitrogen-based fertilizer. Since then much of the world has come to rely on this fertilizer for enhancing crops. Sometimes there can be too much of a good thing. When farmers apply more fertilizer than is needed, the excess eventually becomes runoff and ends up in lakes, rivers, and oceans. The result: explosive algae growth and its deadly consequences.

THE POISONING OF NORTH CAROLINA'S ESTUARY

A string of barrier islands known as the Outer Banks skirts North Carolina's coast and shields the mainland shore from the pounding waves of the Atlantic Ocean. A peaceful shallow lagoon—Pamlico Sound—separates the islands from the mainland. Here freshwater from North Carolina's rivers mixes with salty seawater from the ocean, creating a habitat known as an estuary. Salt marshes fringing the estuary serve as a major nursery for fish, crabs, and oysters that live

Ducks fly alongside a salt marsh.

In the wake of Hurricane Floyd, some hogs managed to survive floodwaters by finding refuge atop their flooded barns.

along the East Coast. The salt marshes also provide a safe haven for throngs of ducks, petrels, shearwaters, and other seabirds.

Occasionally immense storms shatter the tranquility. In September 1999 Hurricane Floyd pummeled North Carolina's coast with fierce winds gusting to 122 miles (196 kilometers) an hour. The fast-moving tempest dumped 15 to 20 inches (38 to 51 centimeters) of rain in a few hours, triggering the worst flooding in North Carolina history. The ground, bloated from a previous hurricane, could not absorb the rain. As water poured from the sky and rolled off the land, streams and rivers turned into raging torrents. Soon riverbanks and stream banks could no longer contain the rampaging currents. The water rushed across the land. Along the way, it sopped up farm fertilizers and lawn chemicals.

Floodwater overran dozens of sewage treatment plants, flushing untreated human waste into the swollen rivers. It tore through junkyards, soaking up oil, gasoline, and battery acid from damaged vehicles. And it inundated poultry farms, drowning about three million chickens and turkeys. Soon rotting poultry carcasses floated across the landscape.

The polluted water reeked and it carried the potential for illnesses, ranging from hepatitis and diphtheria, to tetanus, E. coli, and salmonella poisoning. An even greater environmental threat, however, came from hog-factory farms.

In North Carolina hog farming is big business. Each year about 10 million hogs are raised in the state, most of them in factory farms. A single factory farm contains at least 2 thousand hogs, and each hog produces more than 6 pounds (2.7 kilograms) of urine and feces a day. North Carolina's hogs generate as much sewage each day as do the citizens of New York, New Jersey, Maryland, and Pennsylvania combined. Hog farmers store the raw wastes in *waste lagoons*, titanic-sized open cesspools. During Hurricane Floyd rising waters swamped more than 50 factory farms, killing 30 thousand hogs. Tens of millions of gallons of hog waste spilled out of the cesspools into the deluge.

The filthy floodwater washed into North Carolina's estuary and set the stage for a dead zone. The dissolved nutrients in the water stimulated algae growth at the surface, and when the algae died, they fostered a rapid increase of decay bacteria on the estuary floor. The bacteria also dined on nutrients in the hog manure and other

solid material that had settled to the bottom. As in other dead zones, the decay process robbed the water of its oxygen. Most of the oysters, clams, and blue crabs suffocated in the oxygen-starved parts of the estuary. However, few fish died in the dead zone. Most had fled when freshwater from the first hurricane made the estuary less salty. Many landed in the nets of waiting fishing boats.

OIL SPILLS

Oil spills are another source of pollution that threatens the marine environment. In March 1989 the supertanker *Exxon Valdez*, loaded with about 53 million gallons (200 million liters) of crude oil, set sail from Port Valdez, Alaska. The vessel was headed for a California refinery, where the oil would be turned into gasoline for fuel-hungry cars. But the doomed tanker never reached its destination. Only 25 miles (40 kilometers) out of Valdez, it slammed into a submerged reef and ripped huge gashes in its hull. About 11 million gallons (41,600,000 liters) of thick black oil spewed out of the tanker and into the pristine water of Prince William Sound. This was enough oil to fill around 125 Olympic-size swimming pools.

The oil floated to the surface and rapidly spread out. Attempts to contain it with floating barriers or to break it up with chemicals were all futile. Driven by wind, tides, and currents, the enormous oil slick eventually spanned 460 miles (741 kilometers) southwest from Bligh Reef, the accident site, to Chignik, a small village on the Alaskan Peninsula. But the slick did not drift harmlessly out to the open sea. Instead tides repeatedly washed it ashore. The oil smothered 350 miles (560 kilometers) of the rocky coast with a black, sticky slime. An additional 1,000 miles (600 kilometers) of shoreline were lightly oiled. But the whims of wind and currents left more than 7,000 miles (11,200 kilometers) along the coast untouched.

Workers begin the cleanup of a devastated beach along Green Island, Alaska.

A Mini–Oil Slick

You can see for yourself how oil floats and spreads out on water. Fill a clear bowl with water and then add several drops of vegetable oil. The oil should quickly form a slick with little blobs that break away. Notice that the oil and water don't mix, and the oil remains on top.

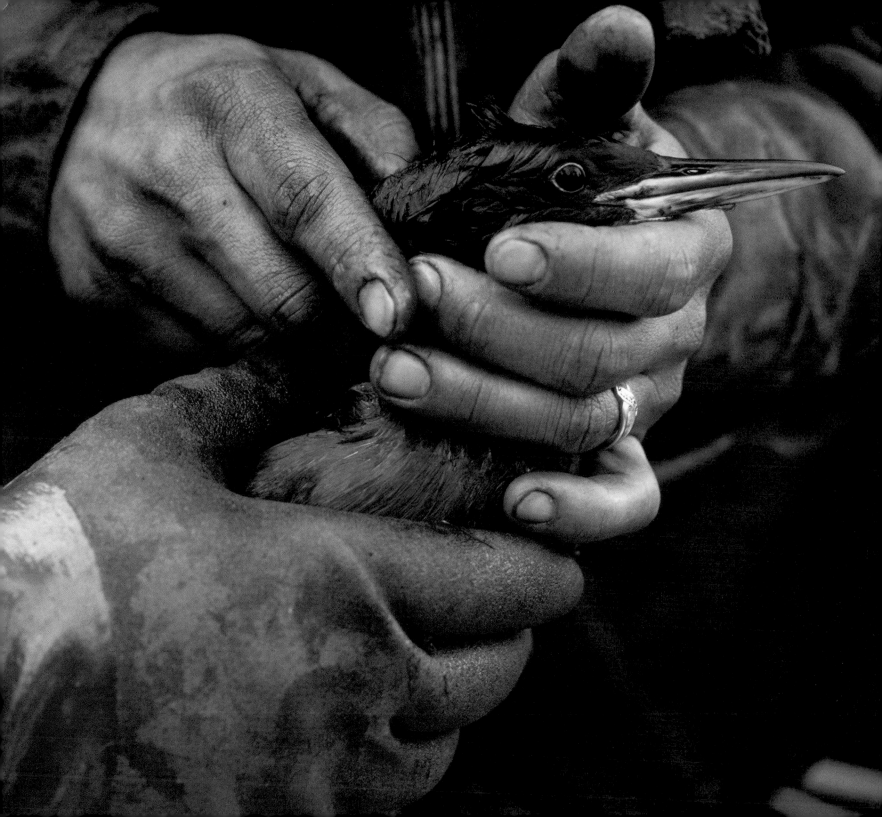

THE COST IN WILDLIFE

No one knows the exact death toll of wildlife since most of the carcasses sank beneath the waves. However, researchers estimate that the oil killed 250,000 seabirds, 2,800 otters, 300 harbor seals, 250 bald eagles, and 14 to 22 killer whales. The oil also clogged some spawning grounds of salmon and herring.

(Left) Rescue workers attempt to save an oil-coated cormorant. The oil ruins the natural water-proofing of feathers and takes away their ability to hold in heat.

(Top) Fur matted with oil loses its ability to trap heat and protect a sea otter from the cold. Many otters that tried to lick their fur clean died from toxins in the oil. Others suffered blindness as well as lung, liver, and kidney damage.

(Above Right) Sea lions sun themselves on an oil-slicked rock formation.

(Below Right) Bald eagles escaped the spill but scavenged the oily dead birds for food for themselves and their offspring—often with fatal outcomes.

15

Exxon initiated a massive cleanup involving 10 thousand people. The process of skimming off oil from open water was painstakingly slow, as was sucking it up with vacuum hoses. On the shore, rakes, shovels, mops, sponges, paper towels, and high-pressure hoses (for blasting hot water over coated rocks) were the weapons at hand. Removing oil that had seeped into the sand proved especially challenging. The recovered oil was recycled and the oil-soaked cleaning materials were burned in incinerators or sent to a toxic-waste dump.

Despite the intensive effort, the cleanup crew was outmatched. The workers succeeded in removing about 20 percent of the spill that came ashore. In the end nature provided the key to recovery. About half of the oil evaporated into the air. Sunlight, oil-eating bacteria, powerful winter storms, and strong wave action broke down and dispersed much of the rest. Interestingly, beaches that had received the most intense cleaning took longer to revive than those that had been left alone. Observers theorize that the heat from the hot water and the stomping of heavy boots did more harm than good to the soil's tiny inhabitants.

Now, more than a decade after the spill, most of the oil has disappeared from all but the smallest bays. Some beaches remain oily, though. Salmon, bald eagles, and river otters have recovered, but the herring, harbor seal, loon, and harlequin duck populations have not.

Since 1970 there have been at least 50 mega-spills involving tankers in which 10 million gallons (37,850,000 liters) or more of oil were lost. However, the *Exxon Valdez* became the ugly symbol for oil spills because it poisoned a wilderness coast prized for its beauty and wildlife.

Cleanup workers scrub rocks on one of the oil-soaked beaches dotting the coast of Naked Island, Alaska.

17

How Oil Is Formed

Oil is a fossil fuel. It formed from the remains of tiny plants and animals that once flourished in shallow ancient seas. When the organisms died, they drifted to the ocean bottom. A layer of mud covered the remains, protecting them from decay bacteria. Over time, sand, more mud, and other sediments wafted down, like snowflakes falling from the sky. New layers of sediment piled up atop the old. The weight of the top layers squeezed the bottom ones, compacting them. Gradually the sediments changed to rocks such as sandstone and shale. The remains became crude oil and natural gas.

The oil and gas rose through the tiny holes in the porous overlying rock. In some places the oil and gas oozed to the surface. In others compact rock, such as shale, blocked the escape and trapped the oil and gas in the porous rock. The oil filled the holes in the porous rock like water fills the spaces in a sponge. Gas which is lighter, collected above the oil. Today much of the world's oil and gas comes from deposits located beneath the shallow coastal waters that rim the continents. Natural seeps, a major source of oil pollution, appear where oil escapes through cracks in the seafloor.

Drilling offshore for oil puts the marine environment at risk for blowouts—uncontrolled releases of oil from wells. In 1979 a blowout in the Ixtoc Field off Mexico's eastern coast hurled 148 million gallons (379 million liters) of crude oil into the Gulf of Mexico.

Most blowouts and oil spills result from accidents, but one of the worst was an act of war. During the Persian Gulf War in 1991, the Iraqi dictator Saddam Hussein deliberately released into the Persian Gulf about 460 million gallons (1,700 liters) of oil from a Kuwaiti oil terminal and five Iraqi oil tankers.

Pollution by the Drop

While spills from oil tankers make headlines, 80 percent of the oil that ends up in the sea originates from other sources. Every day an oil spill in slow motion takes place across America. If you walk in a parking lot after a storm you may spot signs of it—puddles with rainbow-tinted oil swirls. The oil drips from leaky cars and trucks. When rain washes these drippings off roads and other paved surfaces,

Platforms such as this one are used for drilling and pumping oil offshore.

19

the oil flows into storm sewers or waterways. Some eventually winds up in the sea. So many motor vehicles are in operation that oily runoff has become a significant cause of pollution.

Other sources of oil pollution in the ocean include the following:

- used motor oil poured down drains after oil changes
- fuel seeping from underground storage tanks
- oily water dumped illegally from tanks and bilges of ships during cleaning
- unburned fuel discharged by outboard motorboats
- relatively small spills involving tankers, refineries, and offshore drilling operations
- leaks from damaged or sunken ships

Oil swirls on water make a pretty picture, but oily runoff created by oil drippings from motor vehicles detracts from the beauty and health of waterways.

The USS *Arizona* burned and sank during the Japanese attack on Pearl Harbor on December 7, 1941.

Pearl Harbor's Ongoing Oil Leak

On December 7, 1941, Japanese warplanes unexpectedly attacked the U.S. naval base at Pearl Harbor, Hawaii, catapulting the United States into World War II. The savage onslaught severely damaged the U.S. Pacific fleet. Of the approximately 130 ships present, 12 were sunk, including the battleship USS *Arizona.* The commander of the *Arizona,* Rear Admiral Isaac Kidd, perished along with 1,176 other officers and men aboard the battleship. About 333 members of the crew survived the attack. Divers recovered 229 bodies before the navy decided to leave the rest entombed inside the vessel.

For more than 60 years, fuel oil has trickled from the *Arizona* at a rate of about a quart (1 liter) a day. If you visit the USS *Arizona* Memorial at Pearl Harbor you can see the small slick the leak produces. This paltry amount poses little environmental risk, but the estimated .5 million gallons (1.9 million liters) of oil still locked in the wreck could devastate the harbor if it escaped. The lengthy exposure to saltwater has corroded and weakened the ship's metal structure, making a major spill likely.

21

It was once commonly believed that the ocean was essentially a bottomless pit, capable of absorbing all human refuse: any garbage; sewage; industrial, chemical, or military waste disposed of at sea would be quickly diluted to harmless levels, dispersed throughout the ocean and then broken down into its individual components. Although this is true of some wastes, the rest linger much longer, building up in the tissues of sea plants and animals or piling up in the sediments on the seafloor.

The most dangerous refuse in the ocean may be discarded military equipment. The ocean has become a graveyard for relics of modern war. During World War II, thousands of ships sank with their fuel oil and live munitions still intact. For example, the remains of about 40 Japanese ships have lain at the bottom of Truk Lagoon in the South Pacific since the Japanese navy lost a major battle to the United States in February 1944. Coral, sponges, and other sea life have transformed these hulks into picturesque artificial reefs. But their deadly cargo— mines, artillery shells, and other weapons—still remains. Leakage is inevitable as the metal canisters corrode.

The Baltic Sea along the northern coast of Europe became a major dumpsite for bombs, poison gas, mines, grenades, and other weapons captured from German forces by the Allies at the end of World War II. The weapons were loaded onto deteriorating ships, which were then scuttled—sunk at sea—by blowing them up with explosives. No one knows whether or not these drowned arsenals are ticking time-bombs. Danish fishermen have reported more than 150 incidences of chemical weapons being hauled up in fishing nets. Some of the fishermen have been injured.

Chemical weapons have been scuttled in nearly every ocean, and some of the disposal has taken place close to home. In 1967 and 1968 more than 50 thousand nerve-gas rockets were submersed in deep water 150 miles (240 kilometers) from the New York shore. In 1970 nerve gas placed in concrete vaults was sunk off the Florida coast. That year the United States stopped its sea disposal program because of public outcry. In 1972 Congress passed the Marine Protection, Research, and Sanctuaries Act making it illegal to dump chemical, biological, and radioactive warfare agents in ocean waters. It also prohibited the disposal at sea of medical wastes and high-level radioactive waste produced as a result of peacetime uses.

A scuba diver shines a floodlight on the wreck of *Schnellboot 57*, a World War II German torpedo boat sunk off the Croatian coast in 1944 by the British Royal Navy.

chapter 2

SEA SICK

Despite government efforts to safeguard the nation's coastal waters, something nasty is killing fish from North Carolina to Delaware and it has a Dr. Jekyll-Mr. Hyde personality. Usually it munches peacefully on algae and bacteria. But when it senses the presence of large schools of fish, it changes shape and releases a powerful fish-stunning toxin. Then it gives off a second toxin, which splits open fish skin, creating bleeding sores. Finally it eats the fish alive—gorging on blood and tissues.

This unusual killer is millions of times smaller than its prey and it kills in concert with millions of others of its kind. It is Pfiesteria, a type of dinoflagellate. Dinoflagellates are one-celled organisms, usually classified as algae, even though dinoflagellates can swim and some are more animal-like than plantlike.

Pfiesteria toxic feeding-frenzies last a few hours and then the Pfiesteria revert to a harmless form. They have an unusually complex life cycle, existing in at least 24 different guises, of which only a few are lethal. Pfiesteria toxins are so potent that some researchers studying Pfiesteria in a laboratory have become disoriented, developed skin sores, and suffered memory loss.

Pfiesteria are just one of many health threats to sea life today. Other toxin-producing organisms, sewage, garbage and chemical pollutants, can make ocean animals deathly ill.

Toxic Algae Blooms

About 2 thousand different types of dinoflagellates exist. Most are not harmful, but the ones that are have periodically plagued seacoasts for millions of years. Dinoflagellates are always present in seawater, but usually in concentrations so

This paper mill in Saint John's, New Brunswick, is polluting the water, air, and land.

small they pose no danger. Occasionally, however, they reproduce at such a great rate that their populations explode. Then so many organisms appear that they become a threat to fish and other creatures.

As many as 60 million dinoflagellates can populate a single quart (liter) of seawater. The population explosions are known as toxic algae blooms. Sometimes they are called red tides because they can give water a rust-colored appearance. Blooms can be red, green, yellow, brown, orange, pink, or violet. Or they may produce no color changes at all. Whatever the color, blooms of toxic dinoflagellates are responsible for massive fish kills. In 1947 more than 50 million dead and rotting fish piled up on the west coast of Florida as a result of a toxic algae bloom.

Although toxic algae blooms occur naturally, they are becoming more frequent because of pollution. All dinoflagellates, including Pfiesteria, thrive in water polluted by nutrients from farm-animal wastes, fertilizer runoff, industrial waste, and human sewage. In fact the emergence of Pfiesteria in North Carolina's estuary in the late 1980s and 1990s coincided with the growth of the hog industry in the state. (The number of hogs in North Carolina swelled from 2.6 million in 1987 to nearly 10 million by 1997.) In Maryland, where almost 300 million chickens are raised annually, chicken manure contributes to the Pfiesteria problem in Chesapeake Bay.

Some toxic algae blooms can be fatal to even the largest sea creatures. In 1987 dead humpback whales—12 in all—began to wash up on the Massachusetts shore. The humpbacks had feasted on mackerel, fish that swim in large tight schools. The mackerel in turn had fed on toxic dinoflagellates. The toxin apparently had no ill effect on the mackerel because it had collected in low levels inside each individual fish. But the whales had devoured large quantities of the mackerel, each eating perhaps as much as a ton of fish at one meal. The toxins accumulated inside the whales as they digested the fish. The poisons quickly built up to a lethal level, killing the whales.

Some kinds of dinoflagellates can make humans sick. In 1997, 17 crew members of a Norwegian cargo ship fell ill within a few hours of eating a big barracuda. The men complained of nausea, vomiting, dizziness, itching, muscle weakness, and numbness. But their oddest symptom was temperature reversal. Hot things felt cold to the touch and cold things felt hot.

The crew members suffered from ciguatera fish poisoning. Ciguatera toxins originate in a specific dinoflagellate species that lives in tropical waters. Little fish gobble up the dinoflagellates. Larger fish, such as barracuda or snapper, devour the small fish. Although the toxins collect as they ripple through the food chain, they don't appear to hurt the large fish. When humans consume the big fish, trouble begins. The symptoms can linger for several weeks or months. In a few rare cases they persist for years.

Shellfish—scallops, clams, and oysters—can dine on toxic dinoflagellates with no ill effect even though the shellfish retain the toxins in their tissues. If these shellfish are harvested during an algae bloom, the toxin is passed on to the people who eat them. Since cooking does not destroy the poison, the toxin can cause serious illness in humans and, in rare occasions, death. In 1987, the same year in which the whales died, 200 people in Guatemala became extremely ill after eating contaminated shellfish; 26 of them died.

A toxic algae bloom pollutes the coast of the Gulf of Carpentaria edging Queensland, Australia.

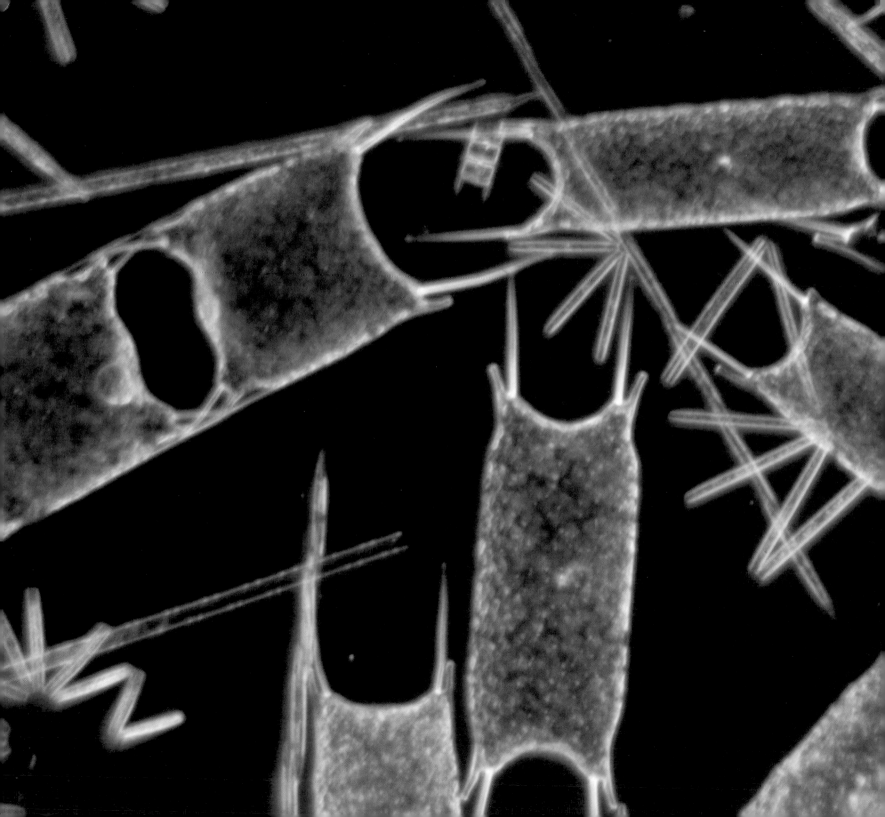

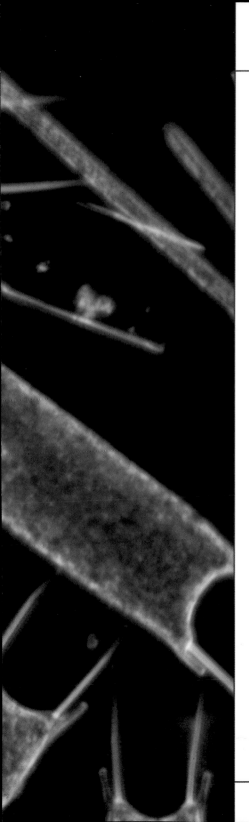

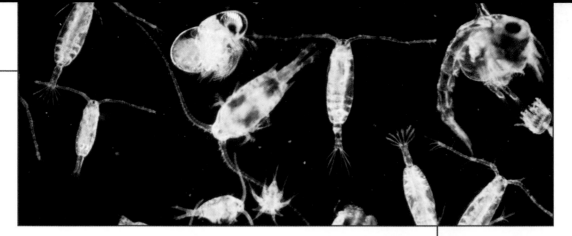

OCEAN FOOD CHAINS

A food chain shows how energy is transferred in the form of food from one organism to another.

(left) Most ocean food chains start with phytoplankton—tiny algae that float in the ocean. Phytoplankton are producers. Like all plants, they capture energy from sunlight and store it in the food they make.

(top) Zooplankton are tiny animals that float freely with the waves and tides. Zooplankton graze on phytoplankton. Like all animals, zooplankton are consumers. They obtain their energy by eating other organisms.

(above right) Caesio bluefish eat zooplankton and are in turn eaten by bluefin Trevally and other predators.

(below right) Hermit crabs, such as the one shown here, and other scavengers eat the leftovers.

UNDERWATER EPIDEMICS

Like Pfiestreria and ciguatera, the bacteria that cause cholera are also ancient organisms with a permanent presence in the sea and the ability to inflict terrible human suffering. The bacteria infect the intestines, causing severe diarrhea, vomiting, and leg cramps. Cholera is spread by ingesting food or water contaminated by the feces of an infected person. The severe diarrhea causes the body to lose so much fluid that a person may die unless treated for dehydration. For the best chance of survival, cholera patients must receive treatment as soon as the first symptons appear. Patients must drink large amounts of clean water containing sugar and certain salts to replace the lost fluids.

During the nineteenth century, six cholera pandemics (worldwide epidemics) began in the Indian Subcontinent and spread outward. Hitchhiking in the gut of an unfortunate sailor, traveler, or immigrant, cholera reached North and South America, where it snuffed out the lives of hundreds of thousands of people. After 1900 improved sewage and drinking-water treatment brought cholera under control, vanquishing it from everywhere but the Indian Subcontinent and parts of Africa.

In 1991 cholera suddenly reappeared in South America and stampeded with a vengeance through the continent. More than 1 million people fell ill, but advances in medicine saved all but 12 thousand. Officials blamed deteriorating water-treatment plants and sewage systems for the spread of the disease. But where did it originate? This cholera strain differed slightly from the strains found elsewhere.

Apparently cholera had never completely disappeared from South America. For nearly a century it had existed quietly in the *cold* waters offshore, waiting for the right conditions to re-emerge. Cholera bacteria cling to the backs of tiny copepods, a kind of zooplankton. Both cholera and copepods need *warm* nutrient-rich water to flourish. In 1991 El Niño provided the missing ingredient. El Niño is a periodic warming in the eastern Pacific Ocean that heats the coastal waters from Ecuador to Chile. These waters, abundant with nutrients from sewage and runoff, then provided the ideal environment for plankton to bloom and cholera to multiply.

Diseases Plaguing Sea Life

Marine diseases are on the rise globally, inflicting pain and death on a large variety of ocean animals:

- Sea turtle populations worldwide are infected with fibropapillomas, noncancerous tumors that grow on the flippers and necks and ultimately suffocate the animals.
- The Taura virus targets shrimps. It turns the tails of its victims pink and is fatal within days. This virus first appeared in Ecuador in 1992 and has wreaked havoc in shrimp farms in Latin America and Texas.
- Dermo and MSX are single-cell parasites that are destroying oyster beds along the East Coast. A similar parasite, dubbed QPX, attacks quahog clams.
- Infectious salmon anemia, a virus that causes uncontrollable bleeding and death in salmon, first surfaced in Norway in 1984. It rampaged through salmon fish farms in Europe, and 13 years later it crossed the Atlantic where it appeared in fish farms in Canada. Eventually it spread to fish farms in Maine.

Sewage

For thousands of years, human sewage has been dumped in the ground or piped into bodies of water. Human wastes, like animal wastes, contain complex molecules made up of nitrogen, phosphorus, and other nutrients. When the human population was small, the environment could recycle the wastes into simpler compounds. But with the growth of cities, natural systems could not absorb it all. In overcrowded areas the soil and water became polluted.

Disease-causing bacteria and viruses burgeon in sewage-laced water, posing a constant threat to people. Unfortunately the link between microbes and diseases was not proven until the nineteenth century. By then epidemics from tainted water had already claimed the lives of countless millions from diseases such as cholera, typhoid fever, hepatitis, and polio.

In 1807 Glasgow, Scotland, was the first city in the world to have filtered drinking water for all its citizens. The first water filtration plant for London, England, followed in 1829, but sewage remained untreated everywhere. By the 1880s, however, cities and towns in Britain were required by law to treat human wastes before disposing of them. A significant number of European cities, especially in Germany, constructed waste treatment plants during the late 1800s and early 1900s. Only a few American municipalities began treating sewage at that time. In the 1920s some major U.S. cities, such as Philadelphia and Chicago, built wastewater treatment plants. Most American cities ignored the problem until after World War II, though, when the federal government subsidized wastewater treatment projects nationwide.

Today most communities in the United States have wastewater treatment plants that process raw sewage in two stages. Primary treatment removes solid matter by passing wastewater through filters and then holding it in tanks until the heavy particles settle out. Secondary treatment brings the filtered liquid into contact with helpful microorganisms, which break down small particles suspended in it. Oxygen may be added to speed up the process. Before the treated water is pumped into a river, lake, or harbor, chlorine is mixed in to kill harmful microorganisms. Unfortunately primary and secondary treatments do not remove dissolved nutrients such as nitrogen and phosphorus.

Some treatment plants process sewage together with runoff carried by storm drains. During heavy rainfalls these plants cannot handle the increased volume and they discharge raw sewage into waterways. Water polluted by harmful microorganisms from raw sewage is the major reason for temporary beach closings.

Municipal treatment plants often receive industrial wastes from factories, many of which use toxic chemicals to produce their products. Typically only a portion of the chemicals are removed from the water. A third step—tertiary treatment—is needed to extract chemical pollutants. An added benefit of tertiary treatment is that it removes dissolved nutrients. However, this treatment is used by less than a third of the treatment plants in the United States because it is too expensive for most cities and towns to afford. As a result, billions of gallons of toxic industrial wastes flow into the nation's waterways annually. Some of these chemical pollutants sink to the bottom of rivers or bays, contaminating the sediments. Others remain in the water. Nevertheless the United States is farther ahead than most nations in regard to wastewater management.

During secondary treatment at this sewage treatment plant, the filtered liquid is sprayed into the air in order to add oxygen.

Despite the proven benefits of wastewater treatment, more than two billion people—a third of the world's population—live in communities with no sewage treatment facilities. Most reside in Africa and southern Asia, where cholera is endemic. Their sewage ends up in local bodies of water, sometimes the same ones where their drinking water comes from.

Filthy Harbors: Canada's Ugly Secret

North of the border, two Canadian cities lag far behind the United States when it comes to sewage treatment. Saint John's, Newfoundland, and Halifax, Nova Scotia, do not even bother to filter their sewage. What gets flushed down a toilet goes straight into their harbors. Although laws exist to promote clean water, the Canadian government has failed to enforce them.

Little has been done in the United States or elsewhere to regulate agricultural runoff, even though it is the driving force behind dead zones. Only 10 percent of the nutrients causing the dead zone in the Gulf of Mexico arises from sewage, industrial wastes, and runoff from streets and chemically treated lawns. The remaining 90 percent originates on farms. What makes this so astounding is that the Mississippi River system (which drains into the Gulf) collects treated wastewater from many major metropolitan areas, including Chicago, Minneapolis-Saint Paul, Denver, Saint Louis, Pittsburgh, Cincinnati, Kansas City, Nashville, and New Orleans, each with a population of more than one million people. If the typical person in each of these locales flushes a toilet five times a day every day for a year, then hundreds of millions of gallons of treated wastewater with its dissolved nutrient load must flow into the Gulf annually. Yet the amount of runoff created by humans is tiny compared to that contributed by crop fertilizers and farm animal wastes.

HEAVY-METAL POISONING

In 1952 the cats living near Minamata Bay, Japan, began to act oddly—drooling, staggering as if drunk, and whirling wildly in circles. Unable to control their movements, some felines even flung themselves into the sea and drowned. Before

Open ditches in Port au Prince, Haiti, carry untreated human wastes. The sewage not only creates a terrible stench but it also poses a serious health threat.

long, dogs and pigs also began to act strangely and birds dropped from the sky in midflight.

By 1956 the bizarre malady began to strike children, and some women gave birth to babies with severe physical and mental disabilities. Soon many adults fell ill. Their limbs and lips went numb, they slurred their words, and their sight diminished. Their bodies shook so uncontrollably, that even the simplest tasks became impossible. Sometimes the disease lead to convulsions and death.

Several years passed before befuddled doctors identified the cause. A local chemical factory had been dumping industrial wastes, including mercury, into Minamata Bay for at least 25 years. The mercury was taken up by plankton in the water. When fish ate the plankton, the mercury became part of their flesh. Inevitably the mercury collected in the tissue of the animals and people who ate the contaminated fish. In 1964 a separate outbreak of Minamata disease occurred along Japan's Agano River. All together, more than 1,400 people died from mercury poisoning and another 11 thousand suffered varying degrees of brain damage and paralysis.

The effects of mercury poisoning have been known for a long time. In the

In April 1993, demonstrators gathered outside a courtroom in Kumamoto, Japan, where the Nippon Chisso Hiryo Company was accused of dumping mercury wastes into Minamata Bay. Many of the demonstrators or their relatives had gotten Minamata disease as a result of the dumping.

37

1800s hat makers—hatters—spread a mercury compound on the felt and fur used in hat production. The mercury killed bacteria and mold, preventing the hats from rotting. But over time the mercury fumes damaged the brains of the hatters. The hatters went "mad," suffering from tremors, slurred speech, severe mood swings, and hallucinations. In *Alice's Adventures in Wonderland,* the author Lewis Carroll may have spoofed the hatters with the Mad Hatter, a jittery character with poor memory and an inability to sleep.

Mercury and other heavy metals such as copper, tin, and iron, occur naturally in the environment. Some are essential minerals required in minute amounts by living things in order to stay healthy. Serious problems arise when heavy metals accumulate in large concentrations in the atmosphere, ground, water, and food chain. High levels can be especially dangerous to humans, as the table below shows.

HEAVY METAL	COMMON SOURCES	DANGER FROM HIGH CONCENTRATION
lead	car batteries, water pipes, lead paint, factories, lead in the gasoline used in underdeveloped nations	toxic to brain—IQ reduction in children, kidney damage
mercury	plastics factories, bread made from grain treated with a mercury-containing antifungal agent (to prevent fungus growth), gold mining	brain and nervous system damage, bone damage, genetic mutations
cadmium	batteries, metal plating, grains and vegetables grown in soil contaminated by mining	cancer, kidney damage, severe bone deformaties
arsenic	contaminated drinking water, mining activity, fossil fuels, some weed killers and pesticides	liver and kidney damage, heart and circulation problems, diarrhea, muscle pains

Toxic POPs

Like heavy metals, manufactured chemicals called POPs (short for *persistent organic pollutants*) can build up to harmful levels as they are transferred up the food chain. In the bodies of humans and animals, POPs mimic the function of hormones—special chemicals made by the endocrine glands. (The endocrine glands regulate many of the body's daily functions as well as long-term growth and development.) POPs can cause cancer, birth defects, developmental problems, and other adverse affects. Among the most dangerous POPs are:

- PCBs—once used to insulate electrical components
- dioxins—by-product of paper manufacturing and the burning of wastes containing chlorine, also used in defoliants
- pesticides—DDT, dieldrin, chlordane, TBT and mirex

POPs persist for a long time in the environment. They are especially dangerous to the unborn of any species, scrambling the genetic information needed for normal development. In Vietnam today some babies are born with missing limbs or eyes that lack pupils. These terrible birth defects are blamed on Agent Orange, a dioxin-containing defoliant sprayed on trees from 1962 to 1969, during the Vietnam War. The defoliant caused leaves to dry and drop, reducing the hiding places of enemy soldiers.

These pollutants can even cause female whelks (a mollusk) to develop male reproductive organs, and they can transform male alligators into females if the alligators are exposed to POPs during a critical period of their development.

POPs can travel thousands of miles from where they were released. The atmosphere even provides a one-way ticket, transporting them from warm climates to cold ones. In the tropics and temperate zones, pesticides and other POPs evaporate from contaminated soils. Winds then whisk them around the world. When they hit cold air near the North and South poles, the pollutants condense and fall as toxic snow or rain.

Near the South Pole, DDT has collected in high levels in the flesh of krill, fish, penguins, and whales that dwell in Antarctic waters. Near the North Pole, seals, whales, and polar bears have high concentrations of PCBs and certain pesticides in their tissues, as do the Inuit people who depend on these animals for food. Although DDT was banned by the United Sates in 1972 and by Canada in 1989, it is still used in some developing countries to combat malaria-carrying mosquitoes.

Many countries do not regulate the use of POPs or cannot enforce existing laws controlling their usage. Even where stringent pollution laws are carried out, problems exist. For example, in some industrialized countries strict air pollution standards reduce the emission of dioxins from incinerators. But the dioxins remain in the ash and when the ash is buried in landfills, they eventually seep out.

PCBs Linked to a Deadly Epidemic in Marine Mammals

In 1990 a virus similar to the ones that cause measles in humans and distemper in dogs began to kill dolphins in the Mediterranean and Ionian Seas. By the time the epidemic ended 3 years later, more than 1,000 dolphins had died. Autopsies showed that extremely high levels of PCBs had accumulated in the blood and livers of the dolphins, enough to damage their immune systems. The impaired immune systems could not fight off the virus infection.

BEACH TRASH

If you walk along any beach, you will probably find trash. The most common items littering the shore are cigarette butts, cans, bottles, plastic six-pack holders, plastic bags, plastic wrap, plastic straws, and paper. Although some of the rubbish comes from careless beachgoers, much is improperly disposed of inland and carried by streams, rivers, and storm drains to the coast.

Plastic debris may look harmless, but it is a deadly menace to ocean life. Each year multitudes of sea animals become entangled in plastic or mistake it for food. Sea turtles eat plastic bags, confusing them with their favorite meal, jellyfish. If the bag doesn't choke the turtle, it may clog the animal's digestive system. Lost or discarded fishing-gear traps whales, seals, and other marine mammals and may slowly cripple or suffocate them. Six-pack yokes ensnare birds and strangle them.

If these Alaskan children follow a traditional Inuit diet, which includes the meat from seals and other Arctic animals, they may have higher concentrations of POPs in their tissues than children in the lower forty-eight states.

This dead South African fur seal was suffocated by plastic that became wound around its neck.

Until recently, waste dumping by ocean-going vessels was a major part of the problem. On any given day, tens of thousands of cargo ships and other vessels are crossing the ocean. However, unlike roadways on land, the great ocean highway doesn't provide rest stops or dumping stations. In the past the ocean, including the great harbors of the world, served as the toilet and refuse heap for ships. Today most ocean dumping is illegal. Yet some rogue vessels illegally discard their wastes at sea to avoid disposal fees charged in ports.

BIOINVASION

Scientists must still tackle the shipping industry's greatest ecological threat— the spread of invasive marine species. An invasive species is an organism that is transported out of its home to a new environment, where it establishes itself and disrupts the existing ecosystem.

Before setting sail, ships with no cargo pick up water to keep them lower in the water and thus more stable. When a ship reaches its destination, it discharges the ballast water as it takes on cargo. More than 80 million tons of ballast are ejected into American waters annually. Unfortunately the water is a virtual aquarium full of bacteria, plankton, small fish, tiny invertebrates, and eggs and larvae of creatures from the ship's point of origin. An environmental crisis begins if this unintended freight establishes itself in the local ecosystem.

Ballast is any heavy material that is used to improve a ship's stability. An empty vessel will carry water in tanks in its lowest part—the bilge— to prevent the ship from riding too high in the water.

In the early 1980s ballast water infected the heavily polluted Black Sea with bell-shaped comb jellies native to North America's Atlantic coast. The comb jellies encountered no natural predators in the Black Sea. With dizzying speed the jellies expanded into a vast alien army, numbering in the billions. Soon they ruled the ecosystem, decimating fish populations by out-competing them for food and eating their eggs and larvae. Ironically in 1997 another stowaway, a different kind of comb jelly, reached the Black Sea in ballast water and is now wolfing down the earlier invader.

Bioinvasion is becoming a leading cause of extinctions worldwide. Ocean ecosystems already weakened by overfishing, habitat destruction, and pollution are at greatest risk. To combat the problem, some nations banned foreign vessels from discharging high-risk ballast in their coastal waters. The ultimate solution lies in science. Researchers are working on ways to sterilize the water before it is released, to destroy potential invaders before they can do harm.

ALIEN SPECIES INVADE U.S. WATERS

- In San Francisco Bay more than 250 marine pests from foreign ports have taken up residence including the aggressive Asian clam, which starves out native species.
- European green crabs with an insatiable appetite for young clams and oysters have invaded some bays in California, Washington state, and British Columbia.
- In 2000, Caulerpa taxifolia—a bright green seaweed from the tropics—was spotted in a lagoon north of San Diego and subsequently destroyed. This fast-moving invader had already carpeted thousands of acres of seafloor in the Mediterranean, smothering everything in its path.
- Since the mid-1980s, European zebra mussels have been squeezing out native mussels in the Mississippi River system and the Great Lakes by competing with them for food. Zebra mussels attach themselves to the shells of native mussels, preventing them from reproducing and eventually suffocating them. Zebra mussels have become a nuisance to boat traffic by affixing themselves to docks, boat hulls, and navigation locks, and they have disrupted water supplies by clogging intake pipes.

FINDING SOLUTIONS TO POLLUTION

Since the 1950s growing awareness of the deadly environmental consequences of human pollution has resulted in significant changes in public policy. In 1970 the federal government established the Environmental Protection Agency (EPA) to identify the impact of pollutants on the environment and to enforce laws to reduce pollution. The Clean Water Act of 1972 was spurred by a burning river.

In 1969 the Cuyahoga River running through Cleveland, Ohio, was so polluted by oil, paint, and other chemicals that fish could not be found in it. That June, sparks from a passing train ignited a floating oil slick. Although the fire blazed for a little over 20 minutes, it inflamed the environmental conscience of the nation. Three years later, Congress passed the Clean Water Act to restore the rivers and streams in the United States and make them safe for fish and wildlife. Since then progress has been made in treating sewage and stopping industrial pollution of waterways. The nation's rivers are cleaner but many are not clean enough. Upgrading sewage treatment plants and controlling runoff, especially from farms, are the next big hurdles.

chapter 3

TOO MANY FISHERMEN

The shimmering blue waters of the ocean cover nearly 71 percent of the Earth's surface. However, if you look at a world map you will most likely see the continents drawn in great detail, while the ocean is depicted as a monotonous blue expanse with no hint of the majestic landscape beneath the waves. If you could explore the vistas on the ocean floor, you would find deeper valleys, wider plains, and mountain ranges longer and more massive than anywhere on land.

You would also discover that the majority of ocean life lives within oyster bays, coral reefs, and other habitats in the shallow water rimming the continents. Impressive as this watery world appears today, it pales in comparison to what it once was. Just three hundred years ago you would have found colossal underwater "cities" packed with sea life along every coast. Overfishing turned many of these lush marine havens into biological deserts.

Overfishing depletes fish stocks by taking fish at a rate faster than they can replace themselves. Many fish are harvested before they are even mature enough to reproduce. As a result, marine species are disappearing at an alarming rate. Some kinds of whales and other sea creatures have already been hunted to extinction. More are on the verge. And development along coasts that drains swamps and fills in wetlands has eliminated precious nurseries for new generations of fish and shellfish.

The same map that gives little information about the ocean realm provides clues about the sea life that previously flourished near shore. Place-names like Cape Cod (Massachusetts), Oyster Bay (New York), Seal Harbor (Maine), and Herring Bay (Maryland) are ghostly reminders of animals once plentiful in these locations.

Historical records provide insight, too. Can you imagine New York's harbor crowded with seals, whales, and porpoises, and its shores teeming with lobsters 6-feet (108-meters) long? The Dutch found such bounty when they settled the region in the early 1600s.

Most people know more about the dinosaurs, which became extinct 65 million years ago, than about the massive sea animals that died out within the last three centuries along their own nation's coasts. However, unlike dinosaurs which will never come back, many sea creatures have a chance of recovery. They are considered to be "ecologically extinct." This means that there are still some left but not enough to make an impact on an ecosystem. Their numbers may increase if they are protected from fishing—commercial as well as sport—and if their habitats are shielded from development and pollution.

Overfishing began in the Stone Age. For example, tens of millions of green turtles once lived in the Caribbean Sea. Now so few remain that the survival of the species is threatened. The turtle decline started three thousand years ago when humans settled the region. The turtles were agile in the water but they made easy prey for hunters when they lumbered up sandy beaches to lay eggs. The people came to rely on turtle meat and eggs as a major part of their diet. On some islands, the turtles disappeared by 800 A.D. From the 1500s on, European

This young green sea turtle has the potential to weigh as much as 300 pounds (137 kilograms) if it lives long enough.

settlers hastened the demise of the remaining turtle populations by harvesting them not only for food, but also for their skin to make leather, and their shells for use in jewelry and other ornaments.

COD AND THE GRAND BANKS

In 1497 explorer John Cabot stumbled upon one of the world's richest fisheries—the Grand Banks off the rocky shores of eastern Canada. Cabot claimed the northern reaches of North America for England, and the grab for fish was on.

The Grand Banks are drowned hills—immense deposits of sand and gravel left by glaciers at the end of the last ice age. Water sweeping over the banks carries nutrients up from the seafloor, encouraging phenomenal growth of phytoplankton floating near the surface. The phytoplankton in turn support an extensive network of interconnected food chains. Along with Georges Bank off New England, the Grand Banks launched a fishing industry that lasted more than four hundred years.

The fish bounty seemed inexhaustible, and of all the fish, cod were the most prized. Cod are large predators that gorge on small fish that travel in schools. Cod prowl the ocean floor for crabs, clams, squid, and lobsters. Not so long ago cod roamed the banks in great herds, like buffalo, but in groups numbering in the hundreds of millions.

At first fishermen used Old World technology to catch the cod. They fished with hooks and hand lines dropped over the sides of small boats. The lines rarely came up empty. Sometimes cod the size of a full-grown man were pulled from the water. In the 1800s many fishers switched to longlines: tar-covered ropes that stretched out a mile. Hundreds of short lines with baited hooks dangled down from the long one. Despite the increased catches, the cod population stayed healthy. The remaining adults produced enough young to replace the ones that were harvested.

The cod fishery on the Grand Banks, off Canada, was not the only one that was overfished. European fishers depleted cod stocks on their side of the North Atlantic as well. In a photograph taken in 1949, a Norwegian fisher displays two of his catch.

However, in 1895 mechanized trawlers changed the balance by taking vast quantities of fish. A trawl is a huge, weighted-down net shaped like a cone. It is dragged across the ocean floor by a boat with a long rope. The trawl scoops up bottom-dwelling fish and crushes or buries everything else in its path. It also eliminates hiding places on the seafloor for surviving creatures, making them more vulnerable to predators.

GOING, GOING, GONE

In the 1950s factory trawlers from Europe and Asia began to fish the Grand Banks. As big as ocean liners, these trawlers were floating fish-processing plants. Their humongous trawling nets spelled doom for the cod. Day and night, for months at a time, these vessels worked the fishing grounds catching, gutting, cleaning, and freezing fish. Sophisticated scanning devices, originally developed to track enemy submarines, were put to work identifying the precise location and size of entire fish schools. The fish were then netted with deadly effectiveness. Year after year these factory trawlers strip-mined the seafloor. They were as devastating to the marine ecosystem as clear-cutting is to a forest.

As time passed, the factory ships increased in number and size. The largest ones dragged nets big enough to hold 12 jumbo jets. Throughout the 1970s cod populations shrank, and the size of individual fish diminished. Eventually the largest cod measured only 12 to 16 inches (30 to 40 centimeters) long. As the fish became harder to find, the demand for them grew, which raised the price. To cash in, more fishing vessels flocked to the Grand Banks. The factory ships also pursued other kinds of bottom-dwelling fish—haddock and yellow-tailed flounder—until their populations collapsed.

In 1977 Canada extended its territorial waters from 12 miles (19 kilometers) to 200 miles (322 kilometers) offshore. The foreign fleets left. But instead of managing its fisheries to ensure cod for the future, the Canadian government provided financial incentives that more than doubled the number of Canadian fishermen and supported the building of a modern trawling fleet.

Traditional Newfoundland fishermen warned that the cod stocks were crashing to dangerously low levels. Scientists at the Canadian Department of

These cod are being raised on a fish farm in the coastal waters of Norway.

Fisheries ignored their warnings, though. By 1992 the nets came up empty and finally the Canadian government closed the fishery.

Canada holds no monopoly on shortsightedness. The Unites States bungled the management of its richest fishing grounds just as badly. Like Canada, the United States extended its territorial waters and banished foreign fleets. The U.S. government then guaranteed loans so the American fishing fleet could replace its rusting boats with fast high-tech ones. Under pressure from the fishing industry to keep the fishing grounds open, the New England Fishery Council squandered its fish stocks. In 1993 the fisheries collapsed and finally were closed.

The cod populations on the Grand Banks and Georges Bank have not rebounded. However, stocks along Newfoundland's southern coast have begun to revive. Perhaps someday they will increase the numbers of cod on the banks. The rebuilding of the cod fishery may take 50 years. With the cod gone, lobsters, clams, and other crustaceans now dominate the ecosystem.

More than 30 thousand people in the Canadian fishing industry lost their jobs, and 14 thousand Americans lost theirs when the fisheries closed. It is almost beyond comprehension why the fishing industry was such an active participant in its own destruction. Part of the problem was that the fish were free for the taking. Perhaps if fishermen had owned a stake in the fishing grounds, they might have valued the stocks more and managed them with an eye on the future. Some governments lease timber rights to lumber companies and grazing land to ranchers. Why not sell shares of fisheries? Fish stocks can be a renewable resource if given the opportunity to rebuild their populations.

Sadly, what happened on the banks is not unique. As fisheries become barren, factory fleets move on to new ones and deplete the fish there. International fishing has become the new gold rush. Enterprises eager to make a profit grab whatever they can and ignore the wreckage they leave behind. Of the world's 17 major fishing grounds, 4 have already been fished out. Nine are in serious danger. Fishers from poor countries cannot compete with the foreign factory vessels that empty local fishing grounds. Too often, corrupt government leaders of poor nations sell fishing rights to rich countries and pocket the money. This adds to the hunger and poverty of local people dependent on the fish.

Fishing Down the Food Chain

Once the largest fish—the top predators in an ecosystem—are removed, fishers target the next largest species in the food chain. With each step lower in the food chain, the fish become smaller and more abundant. Species regarded previously as "trash" fish because they are small and bony now grace the plates of diners in even the priciest gourmet restaurants. Fishers also harvest fish that don't appeal to human tastes and sell them as bait, fertilizer, and pet food. This removal of vast quantities of fish lower down the food chain robs big fish of prey and hinders the recovery of threatened species.

An abundant supply of unpolluted water is a necessity for inland fish farms.

FISH FARMING

If you have eaten trout or salmon, chances are it was raised on a fish farm. As wild fish stocks have decreased, aquaculture—fish farming—has increased. Numerous fish farms have been built inland, far from the sea. Catfish are raised

in shallow ponds in the southern states. The world's biggest trout farm is in Idaho.

Salmon are raised in enclosed floating pens along the shores of the Pacific Northwest and New England. Mussels, clams, and oysters are also farmed in coastal waters. Like livestock, these fish and shellfish are grown in large numbers under controlled conditions.

Marine aquaculture has its pluses and minuses. It provides steady employment and offers a year-round supply of fresh seafood. But excess fish feed and wastes from penned-in fish can generate algae blooms, which can deplete the oxygen in the water when they decay. Disease outbreaks are more likely in captive populations and may spread outside the pens. Good management and placing pens in an area with a steady current can overcome these problems. Done properly, aquaculture has the potential to provide much-needed food for humans while sparing the natural environment.

BIODIVERSITY: EARTH'S GREATEST TREASURE

Overfishing sends shock waves through an ecosystem. Since each kind of organism is adapted to living with others in its environment, when one form of life vanishes, others are impacted. An entire ecosystem can break down if a keystone species disappears. A keystone species is essential to the survival of other kinds of organisms in its habitat.

The ecosystem in Chesapeake Bay collapsed when too many oysters were removed. Adult oysters look like misshapen clams. They spend their lives in brackish partly salty water attached to a hard surface, such as a rock or another oyster shell. They often live in immense clusters called beds or reefs. The reefs provide shelter for rockfish (striped bass), shad, blue crabs, sturgeons, and numerous other species. When the reefs disappeared from the Chesapeake, so did much of the sea life dependent on them.

No one knows for sure how many different kinds of organisms live in the ocean. But protecting the sea's biodiversity—its rich variety of life—is a major challenge facing humanity. To keep an ecosystem healthy, every population within it must have a rich diversity of genetic traits. Genetic traits determine an individual's characteristics, such as eye color, capacity to digest specific foods, and the ability to ward off different diseases.

Each organism carries its genetic traits within the chromosomes inside its cells. You have 26 chromosomes: 13 from your mother and 13 from your father. They serve as blueprints that control how your cells make and shape each tissue and organ in your body. You have many genetic traits—genes—in common with other humans, but you also have some genes that differ. Except for identical twins, no two individuals have exactly the same set of genes.

Your genes are part of the human gene pool. A gene pool contains genes for all the traits of all the members of a specific population. Without genetic diversity, a species is less able to adapt to diseases or changes in its environment.

A healthy marine ecosystem is better able to cope with stresses from pollution, overfishing, bioinvaders, and climate change than an ecosystem that lacks biodiversity. Unfortunately too many marine ecosystems have been stressed by human activities.

Earth is now undergoing the greatest die-off of species since dinosaurs became extinct. Half the species living today may vanish within the next 50 years. As ecosystems and the life they support decline and disappear, their resources— which humans depend on—are lost.

No one knows for sure what this means for humanity or for the organisms that share the planet with us. We are in the midst of a huge uncontrolled experiment. However, unlike other species, we have the ability to change the course of events, and it is not too late.

Working together, the nations of the world can save the creatures of the sea. International agreements have already restricted the killing of whales and seals, allowing many of these marine mammal populations to partially recover and stabilize.

The best hope for reviving marine ecosystems may be marine parks and sanctuaries that prohibit fishing. Free from hooks and nets, no-fishing zones have not only restored marine populations within the reserves, but the fish have spread out and replenished the surrounding waters. Less than 1 percent of the ocean has been set aside as safe havens. We need more of them.

chapter 4

THE IMPACT OF GLOBAL WARMING

Off the northeast coast of Australia lies the Great Barrier Reef, a 1,250 mile-long (2,000 kilometer-long) "apartment complex" in the sea. There, shimmering schools of brightly colored fish dart in and out of nooks and crannies. Octopuses hide in underwater caves waiting to ambush passing crabs and fish. Barracuda stalk the channels hunting for herring and mackerel. Rippling with life, the reef provides food and shelter for more than a thousand different kinds of fish, sponges, starfish, and mollusks.

The Great Barrier Reef is one of the largest natural structures on Earth. If you plunked it on top of the United States, it would extend from New York City to Chicago. Despite its behemoth size, the reef owes its existence to trillions of tiny coral polyps, cousins of jellies.

The polyps form hard outer shells to surround their soft bodies. Corals live in large groups fastened to each other by their shells. When corals die, their shells remain in place and new corals build their homes on top of them. Over thousands of years this process creates reefs that may extend hundreds of miles.

Coral polyps are transparent sacs with a mouth at one end surrounded by waving tentacles. Polyps use their tentacles to catch zooplankton. Polyps cannot capture all the food they need, though. So they host single-celled algae that live within their tissues and give the reefs their brilliant color. The algae carry out photosynthesis and provide nutrients to the corals. The corals, in turn, give the algae a safe place to live.

Although hard as rock, coral reefs are fragile. They can grow only in clear, shallow tropical waters. And they can survive only within a narrow temperature range. Unfortunately the impact of human activities has destroyed more than 25 percent of the world's reefs. Sewage that clouds the water prevents sunlight from reaching the corals. Eroded soil washed down from adjacent landmasses smothers the polyps. In some places fishers dynamite reefs or poison them with cyanide to force fish to the surface.

Bleached coral

The greatest menace, however, is global warming—the gradual increase in the average world temperature. During the twentieth century the average global temperature rose about 1 degree Fahrenheit (0.6 degree Celsius), the largest increase in at least one thousand years. This may not seem like much, but some places grew warmer than others. Certain tropical seas became hot enough to cause coral bleaching: the reefs heated up and the corals expelled their algae. When the water got too hot, the corals died. In the Indian Ocean, some islands have lost about 90 percent of their reefs.

GLOBAL WARMING IS HERE TO STAY

Unless you are one of the millions of people who depend on fish from coral reefs for your protein, why should you care about global warming? Global warming is the greatest climatic change that Earth has experienced in the past 10 thousand years. Eventually it will impact everybody, including you. Global warming is already causing the widespread melting of mountain glaciers far from the poles and the thawing of the permafrost (permanently frozen soil) near the North Pole.

An amazing string of weather calamities occurred during the 1990s, and some scientists blame global warming:

- In 1992 a powerful Nor'easter blindsided New York City, flooding lower Manhattan Island and its underground subway system.
- A killer heat wave in the summer of 1995 snuffed out the lives of approximately 525 people in Chicago.
- In January 1998, an unprecedented five-day ice storm struck upper New York State, northern New England, and Quebec. It glazed buildings, trees, roads, and utility wires with an ice coating up to 4 inches (10 centimeters) thick.
- Later that year, Hurricane Mitch stalled for five days over Central America, dumping 1 to 2 feet (30 to 60 centimeters) of rain a day in mountainous regions. Floods and mud slides swept away entire villages and killed an estimated 11,000 people in Honduras and Nicaragua.

This is just the beginning. With rising temperatures, more water will evaporate from the ocean into the atmosphere. Additional moisture in the air means bigger and more ferocious storms. Temperature and rainfall patterns will shift. So the weather you experience now may be much different in the future. Longer droughts, more gruesome floods, and wilder hurricanes will occur. Potentially deadly diseases such as West Nile virus and dengue fever, once confined to the tropics, will become more widespread.

During the twentieth century, global warming caused the sea level to rise 4 to 10 inches (10 to 25 centimeters). Climate experts predict that the sea level could climb an extra 4 to 35 inches (9 to 88 centimeters) over the next 100 years, depending on how quickly Earth's atmosphere warms. They also expect the average global temperature to increase 2.2 to 10 degrees Fahrenheit (1.4 to 5.8 degrees Celsius). The additional heat will shrink glaciers and ice caps, releasing enough water for the phenomenal sea-level rise. Much of the water will come from the ice sheet covering Greenland.

Tens of millions of people live in low-lying areas that are likely to be flooded. Among the most threatened places are Bangladesh, the Netherlands, and the densely populated coasts of India, Egypt, and China. What will happen to the people who make their homes there? If you live beside the sea, you may need to move. A rise of just 19 inches (50 centimeters) could swamp coastal cities such as New York, Boston, New Orleans, London, Venice, and Shanghai.

A QUICK LOOK AT PLANETARY HEATING

Blanketing the Earth is an invisible ocean—the atmosphere—and the air you breathe is part of it. Although the atmosphere stretches more than 375 miles (600 kilometers) high, three-fourths of its particles are squished at the bottom in a layer 5 to 9 miles (8 to 14.5 kilometers) thick. All weather takes place in this lowest layer.

Like the ocean of water, the ocean of air moves continually. Both "dance" to the same "music"—the Sun's energy and Earth's gravity—and their steps are intertwined. The daily rhythm begins with sunlight beating down on the Earth's surface, heating the land and sea. In turn, the land and sea radiate some of their heat, warming the air close above them. Warm air expands and becomes lighter. Balloonlike, it rises above the Sun-heated surface. Cooler, heavier air sinks down to take its place. At the surface of the sea, winds blowing horizontally power the ocean's waves and surface currents.

The Sun heats Earth's surface unevenly. The most obvious difference is as apparent as night and day: the Sun shines on only half the planet at a time. The side facing the Sun receives sunlight, while the side facing away gets none. The half in darkness loses heat. So nighttime temperatures are typically cooler than daytime.

Even in daylight, some parts of the Earth's surface receive more energy than others. The tropics—the area around the equator—bask in the most sunlight. The poles receive the least. Consequently, tropical waters are quite warm and polar waters are bitterly cold.

Despite the temperature extremes, the ocean is an enormous reservoir for the Sun's heat. It drinks up the excess heat of summer and slowly lets it go in winter. The ocean also has an astonishing capacity to move this heat over tremendous distances. Currents—gigantic "rivers" that churn through the ocean—serve as planetary conveyor belts. They transfer warm water from the tropics toward the poles and carry cold water back from the poles to the tropics. As a result the ocean redistributes Earth's heat and governs its climates.

Until recently Earth's ecosystems were in sync with the rhythms of their climates. For the most part, climatic changes occurred so slowly that plants and animals could adapt. But global warming is changing the dance. Planetary heating is out of step with the rest of the planet. It is moving too quickly for some species to keep up.

At the end of the twentieth century, global warming triggered a severe food shortage for some penguin species near Antarctica. Penguins eat krill, tiny shrimplike animals that subsist on diatoms. Diatoms are tiny, one-celled algae that are enclosed by a glass shell. Some kinds of diatoms grow on the underside of pack ice—ice that floats in the water surrounding Antarctica. Normally pack ice extends over the ocean for long distances in winter. But in recent years warming seas prevented the water from freezing as far north as usual. Without the pack ice and its diatoms, the krill had no food. The krill died and then the penguins

Global warming may cause
the extinction of Magellanic
penguins as well as other
penguin species.

began to starve. Now, 10 out of the 17 penguin species are in danger of extinction.

THE RELATIONSHIP BETWEEN WEATHER AND CLIMATE

Weather changes from day to day, season to season. The climate of an area describes its weather patterns over a long period of time. People expect variety in their weather, even if the changes include an occasional dry spell or unrelenting rainfall. However, they also expect the overall climate to remain the same. Yet Earth's history reveals a different picture. Over the eons, the world has endured many ice ages—times when ice cloaked up to a third of the land. Periods of warming alternated with ice ages.

Climate experts can't say for sure why Earth's climate swings back and forth. According to the most widely accepted theory, regular fluctuations in Earth's rotation and orbit affect the amount of sunlight reaching the planet. This seesawing between ice ages and warm periods is inevitable and part of Earth's natural climate rhythm. However, the rapid global warming taking place now is not part of that rhythm.

This power plant in Orebro, Sweden, burns oil.

The Greenhouse Effect

The amount of solar energy absorbed by Earth's surface and atmosphere are key factors in regulating Earth's temperature. But not all of the solar energy that hits the atmosphere is absorbed. Clouds, gas molecules, and even the ground and ocean bounce some of the incoming sunlight back into space.

The sunlight that is absorbed by the planet's surface changes into infrared energy (heat), which warms the land and sea. The land and sea radiate much of the heat energy upward into the atmosphere. Some of the heat energy zips directly into outer space. But heat-absorbing gases in the atmosphere, such as water vapor and carbon dioxide, trap the rest. These gases become warmer when they absorb heat energy. In turn, they warm the surrounding air and also radiate some heat back toward Earth's surface.

The heat-absorbing gases are called greenhouse gases. The role they play in atmospheric warming is known as the greenhouse effect. The greenhouse effect is vital for the survival of humans and most other living things. Without greenhouse gases, Earth's surface temperature would plummet far below freezing. The entire planet surface would ice over.

The Carbon Cycle Swings Out of Balance

Nature is in the recycling business. It routes carbon dioxide through the environment as part of the carbon cycle. Carbon is an element that makes up less than 1 percent of all matter. Yet it is a basic building block of life—a necessary ingredient of the complex molecules needed to form cells and carry out life functions. All organisms, including you, serve as living warehouses for carbon. Forests are exceptionally large repositories, holding vast amounts of carbon in their wood. When an organism dies and decays, its carbon may reenter the environment as carbon dioxide.

The carbon cycle starts with volcanoes belching out carbon dioxide from Earth's molten interior. During an eruption, carbon dioxide—along with other gases dissolved in magma—escapes into the air.

Plants play a crucial, but complicated, role in the carbon cycle. During the day plants suck in carbon dioxide and water and use sunlight to convert them into glucose, a sugar. Plants produce oxygen as a by-product. You know this amazing feat as photosynthesis. At night, in a process called cellular respiration, plants

snatch back some of the oxygen. Their cells use the oxygen to release the energy in some of the glucose. The cells require this energy to perform life functions, such as growing new leaves. During respiration, plants give off carbon dioxide as a waste product. Nevertheless, plants consume more carbon dioxide during photosynthesis than they release into the atmosphere during respiration. This makes plants good storehouses for carbon dioxide.

In the atmosphere, some carbon dioxide is dissolved by water. It forms a weak acid called carbonic acid, which falls as acid rain. (You know carbonic acid as the invisible substance that makes soft drinks fizzy.)

In the ocean, corals use carbonic acid to make calcite shells. The shells remain part of the reef after the corals die. A reef can stay intact for millions of years without living polyps. Eventually, if sediments bury a coral reef, the calcite shells may turn into limestone. Limestone locks up much of the carbon on Earth's surface. Limestone on the seafloor is recycled along with the ocean floor and returned to the planet's molten interior. There the limestone melts and recycles into carbon dioxide again.

Seafloor Spreading

The ocean floor is recycled in a process called seafloor spreading. Volcanoes give birth to the seafloor at the mid-ocean ridge, an underwater mountain range that winds through the basins of the world's oceans. Here molten rock from beneath Earth's crust bubbles up through a rift—a long crack—spreads out, and hardens. More molten rock spurts up through the crack, splices the recently hardened rock, and pushes it to each side of the ridge. This process continually creates new strips of seafloor. Each strip of seafloor gradually moves farther and farther away from the ridge. Eventually it meets its death in a deep-sea trench, where it is pulled down into hot molten rock and melts. The entire cycle from birth to death takes about 200 million years.

Coal, oil, and natural gas also store enormous amounts of carbon because they were formed from the remains of ancient organisms. The burning of fossil fuels converts the carbon back into carbon dioxide. For 10 thousand years the carbon cycle stayed in balance. As much carbon entered the atmosphere as was withdrawn. But the excessive burning of fossil fuels to power motor vehicles, run industrial machinery, generate electricity, and heat or air-condition buildings disrupted this balance. So much carbon dioxide has been released into the atmosphere that it has turned the beneficial greenhouse effect into the global-warming threat.

UNDERGROUND COAL FIRES MENACE THE CLIMATE

Underground coal fires are a significant source of carbon dioxide, especially those in China, where the fires may consume as much as 100 to 200 million tons of coal a year. The Chinese subterranean blazes probably account for 2 to 3 percent of all the carbon dioxide released into Earth's atmosphere by the burning of fossil fuels. Coal fires erupt naturally when wildfire ignites an exposed coal seam deposit at the surface or lightning strikes a tree and chars the underground root system. Human carelessness can spark coal fires, too.

Coal fires occur most frequently in areas of active mining. Under the right conditions, coal can burst into flames spontaneously when exposed to oxygen, especially if coal dust is present. Open tunnels and cracks in the coal seams channel oxygen to the flames.

Underground fires not only waste an important energy source and produce carbon dioxide, but they also release toxic gases, heat the overlying ground, burn vegetation and nutrients in the soil, and cause land to sink. The fires pose a serious hazard not only in China, but in other coal-rich countries, including India, Indonesia, South Africa, Australia, and the United States. Despite the danger, miners work alongside burning rock in some open-pit mines in China and India.

Once a buried fire spreads significantly it becomes extremely difficult to extinguish. Large coal deposits can smolder for decades or centuries. A fire in Australia's aptly named Burning Mountain has been burning continuously for one thousand years or more.

In the United States, the best publicized mine fire has been simmering beneath Centralia, Pennsylvania, for more than 40 years. The fire started in 1962 when someone apparently tossed burning trash into an abandoned mine shaft used as a garbage dump. By 1984, the danger from toxic fumes, cave-ins, and

houses catching fire prompted the federal government to set aside $42 million to relocate the town's 1,100 residents. By 1990 all but 63 townspeople had left. Unchecked fires are slowly consuming coal in nearly 50 other abandoned mines in Pennsylvania. Coal fires have been a problem in West Virginia, Wyoming, Utah, Colorado, and Kentucky, too.

Researchers are experimenting with different ways to snuff out the coal fires. They have successfully extinguished small fires by drilling holes in the ground and pumping in foam or gases that won't burn. Damming streams to flood the ground overlying the fires has also worked. Even if all the coal fires could be extinguished, it would solve only a small part of the global-warming problem.

TURNING DOWN EARTH'S THERMOSTAT

To treat Earth's planetary fever, scientists are investigating ways to pull carbon dioxide from the atmosphere and stow it out of harm's way. Under the fancy name of *carbon sequestration,* various strategies have been proposed.

Coal, dirt, and flames spout from the Earth as miners blast and load coal at a strip mine near Wright, Wyoming. Unlike natural fires in underground coal deposits, these flames are easily contained.

69

One plan would use algae as a gigantic sponge to soak up carbon dioxide from the atmosphere. The idea is to scatter tiny bits of iron over barren stretches of the ocean, where they will act as a fertilizer and spur algae growth. The growing algae would sop up billions of tons of carbon dioxide and keep it in their cells. Theoretically when the algae died, they would drop to the depths. Their carbon-rich remains would then become part of the ooze on the seafloor and over time turn into limestone sediments.

Another sequestering plan would tap the sea's tremendous carbon-storing capacity. The atmosphere naturally cycles about 80 percent of its carbon dioxide into the ocean. This scheme would simply enhance the process. Specially designed ships could pump cold pressurized carbon dioxide into the ocean through pipes 2 miles (3.2 kilometers) long. The carbon dioxide would sink to the deep ocean floor where it would stay for centuries. (Little mixing takes place between the top and bottom layers of the ocean.) Ultimately the gas would work its way to the surface and into the atmosphere again, creating a problem for future generations.

A third approach to carbon storage utilizes depleted coal mines and oil fields. Pressurized carbon dioxide is already used to flush oil from remote underground pockets and to force natural gas out of coal seams. This technology could be adapted to inject carbon dioxide into the porous rocks that once trapped oil and gas. Stowing carbon dioxide underground could be risky. Carbon dioxide is heavy and deadly. If an earthquake cracked open the ground and the gas escaped, it would spread out in a toxic, ground-hugging cloud.

Something similar occurred in western Africa at Lake Nyos in Cameroon. The lake filled a deep crater at the top of a volcano. Over the years, carbon dioxide seeped up from the volcano and collected in the lake bottom. One night in 1986 something stirred up the water, unleashing a deadly cloud of carbon dioxide. Without warning, the odorless cloud rolled down the flanks of the volcano and suffocated 1,700 humans and 3,000 animals.

Some researchers are working on designs for immense scrubbers to suck carbon dioxide from the sky. One possible scrubber would consist of towers that spew out a continual mist of calcium hydroxide droplets. The droplets would react with carbon dioxide, producing calcite. Too heavy to stay aloft, the calcite would fall to the ground, where it would be collected. The carbon dioxide would then be removed and stored in the ocean or underground, and the calcium hydroxide would be recycled.

Other investigators are experimenting with ways to strip carbon dioxide from power plants and automotive exhaust before it is released into the air. Some are even looking into the possibility of separating carbon from fossil fuels before they are burned. The technological hurdles and the environmental impact of these methods must be worked out before any of them can be implemented on a large scale.

CARBON FARMING

In the meantime stockpiling more carbon in plants and soil may slow global warming. Improved agricultural techniques can pull vast amounts of carbon dioxide from the air and tuck them away in the ground. Traditionally, after harvesting a crop, farmers plow under the leftover stems and stalks, leaving soil exposed. This is called tilling. Carbon dioxide readily escapes from the bare dirt. With no-till farming, farmers leave the plant stubble in place and sow the seeds for the next crop directly through it.

This low-tech solution drastically reduces the amount of bare ground and hinders the release of carbon dioxide. As the stubble deteriorates, it actually puts carbon back in the soil. Banking carbon in soil is just a short-term fix, though. Soil can hold only a limited amount of carbon. With these farming methods, soil will reach its carbon dioxide-storing capacity within 25 to 50 years.

Another low-tech tactic for stowing carbon is the Johnny Appleseed approach—plant new forests and delay the harvesting of mature ones. But this is not a long-term solution either—carbon dioxide absorption declines as trees mature. There is also the risk of forest fires, which can liberate immense amounts of carbon dioxide into the atmosphere.

In the short run, reducing the consumption of fossil fuels is the best way to trim carbon dioxide production. This can be done by:

- reducing the amount of energy used in the home, in the workplace, and by vehicles
- increasing the energy efficiency of cars, appliances, and electronic equipment
- generating electricity from natural gas instead of coal because gas is lower in carbon than coal

These stopgap solutions may buy enough time until a permanent solution is implemented—switching completely to alternative energy sources such as nuclear power, solar energy, wind energy, geothermal energy, tidal power, and hydrogen fuel cells (whose only by-product is water).

In the year 2000, wind farms in California produced enough electricity to supply 1.3 million households.

chapter 5

THE HUMAN FOOTPRINT

You share living space on planet Earth with more than 6 billion other people. This number is so huge it is nearly impossible to comprehend. But if you had a dollar bill for each person, the bills laid end to end would extend about 579,500 miles (933,000 kilometers), more than twice the distance between the Earth and the Moon. The existence of so many humans is already straining Earth's resources, including the oceans of the world. Yet every minute of every day the human population continues to enlarge.

Life on Earth exists in the biosphere, a zone about 12 miles (19 kilometers) thick, stretching from the bottom of the deepest ocean to the peak of the highest mountain. A myriad of different ecosystems form the biosphere such as rain forests, deserts, and tundra on land; and estuaries, oyster bays, and coral reefs in the sea. Each ecosystem is a distinct community of plants, animals, and microorganisms along with their nonliving environment.

Within an ecosystem all the members of the same species make up a population. Populations increase when more individuals are born than die. They shrink when more members die than are born. Populations also change in size when individuals move in or out.

Every ecosystem has a carrying capacity—the largest population that it can support. In ocean ecosystems population sizes are limited by light, nutrients, food, predators, toxins, salinity, temperature, water pressure, and availability of dissolved oxygen. Many scientists think that Earth has already reached its carrying capacity for human beings. Today at least 2 billion people live in poverty so extreme they cannot obtain enough food and water to keep healthy or work productively.

Beachgoers have flocked to the coast at Quing Dao, China.

BIG TROUBLE FOR BIG FISH

These fish will face ecological extinction unless fewer are taken from the sea.

(left) Shark-fin soup is considered a delicacy and status symbol in the Far East. A bowl of it can cost as much as $100 in Hong Kong. About 100 million sharks a year are killed to meet this demand. Poachers slice the fins off living sharks and then toss the maimed fish back into the sea to die.

(above right) Before their stocks were plundered, swordfish weighing 600 pounds (270 kg) could be found in the seas. Today the average swordfish sold tips the scales at 60 pounds (27 kg) and is still immature. Female swordfish don't reproduce until they weigh about 150 pounds (68 kg). The youngsters found in fish markets have not even had a chance to reproduce.

(below right) A full-grown bluefin tuna can weigh as much as 1500 pounds (680 kg) and measure 6 feet (2 m) long. Prized as sushi, most bluefin tuna wind up in Japanese fish markets. There a single fish can reel in more than $90,000. As a result, bluefin tuna populations have tumbled nearly 90 percent since the 1970s. No government has ordered a stop to the slaughter. Part of the problem is that the tuna travel thousands of miles and do not stay within the territorial waters of a single nation. Another is the ease with which bluefin tuna caught in New England waters can be delivered live the next day to Tokyo's fish market, half a world away.

Overpopulation

Earth wasn't always so crowded. The human population didn't reach the 1 billion mark until 1800 or so. By 1957 it was nearly 3 billion. Between 1987 and 1999 it leaped from 5 billion to 6 billion. Today population growth has stabilized in nearly all industrialized countries, but the numbers continue to skyrocket in developing nations. Guatemala, Laos, Pakistan, and Iraq have a birthrate of five or six children per woman. Most African nations have an even higher one.

If present growth trends continue, the world population will balloon to nearly 8 billion people by 2025, and 9 billion by 2050. Some scientists think that the population will peak at around 9 billion, but no one knows for sure.

How will the needs of 3 billion more individuals be met in the future when we cannot adequately feed one-third of the people alive today? One thing is certain: the planet's ecosystems will be severely impacted.

Curbing Human Population Growth

In 1964 when civil rights leader, Martin Luther King, Jr., accepted the Nobel Peace Prize, he said, "I have the audacity to believe that peoples everywhere can have three meals a day for their bodies, education and culture for their minds, and dignity, equality, and freedom for their spirits."

To help make King's dream a reality, the upward spiral in world population must be halted. Families in poor nations typically produce more children than ones in wealthy nations. Ironically, extremely large families are the most common in the countries with the least amount of food. In these places children are often valued for their labor as farmhands or factory workers. Unlike children in America, these child workers have no time for play and no opportunity to attend school to prepare for their future. In India alone, approximately 50 million children work in factories, mostly in the carpet-making industry. Although their wages are extremely low, the children serve as an important income source for their households.

Reducing poverty is the most humane way to slow population growth and improve the quality of life in poor nations. This involves expanding educational and economic opportunities for both men and women, and providing access to family planning. It also entails changing social attitudes. Where children are regarded as an investment in the future, smaller families usually result and each child is given greater opportunities. The payoff comes after the children finish school and land better-paying jobs.

Other forces affect human population growth. Unfortunately war, genocide, terrorism, civil strife, famine, natural disasters, and infectious diseases—including the HIV/AIDS epidemic in Africa—serve as population checks, too. Government intervention, such as China's one-child policy, may be imposed on the citizens of an overpopulated country. China's one-child policy is an extreme measure that was taken in 1979 to regulate China's skyrocketing population growth. In return for agreeing to have only one child, married couples and their child were granted educational and economic benefits.

PRESSURE ON COASTAL ECOSYSTEMS

Today roughly 60 percent of the global population—an astounding 3.6 billion people—live within 40 miles (60 kilometers) of the seashore. By the year 2030, the coastal population is expected to double. That means more than 6 billion people—the number of people alive today—will crowd the narrow ribbons of land edging the oceans. This expansion will take place at the same time that shorelines will be threatened by rising seas due to global warming.

If you look at a world map, you will see that two-thirds of the largest cities are nestled next to rivers adjacent to the sea. These urban areas serve as economic engines for their countries, generating new businesses and trade with other nations. In turn the new businesses and increased trade create more jobs and wealth.

The cities spread out along large harbors that once served as spawning areas and nurseries for a rich variety of fish and shellfish. The qualities that make these harbors so appealing to humans—shelter from pounding ocean waves and close-ness to rivers—also make superior habitats for sea life. However, the estuaries,

swamps, and marshes in these harbors lost out to the human demand for ports, manufacturing, energy production, and living space. Developers filled in wetlands to make shorelines more compatible with human goals, destroying significant natural habitats in the process.

The downside of development is not limited to urban areas. To make room for cropland, vacation homes, resorts, marinas, golf courses, and other human uses, wetlands have been decimated worldwide. Ironically, as development increases, the remaining natural assets that attract people to the shore may vanish.

Marine habitats are at exception-ally high risk in developing countries. Because resources are often scarcer in nations where poverty and hunger are widespread, growing coastal populations put more pressure on the ocean environment. People chop down mangrove forests for lumber and firewood, break up coral reefs to manufacture concrete, and create more stress on fisheries. As more of humanity becomes dependent on the ocean for food and work, more habitat destruction will follow. More pollution will be generated.

A helicopter view of San Francisco

81

Mangrove Forests

Mangroves are stumpy gnarled trees that thrive in brackish water along the coast. Anchored to the soil by strong roots, these trees can survive all but the most powerful of hurricane winds. The area around their roots provides a critical nursery habitat for countless fish, shrimps, crabs, and other creatures. Their canopies shelter a wide variety of birds. In parts of Southeast Asia, man-eating crocodiles make their homes in mangrove forests.

OVERCONSUMPTION

Pinning all of Earth's woes on overpopulation and poverty masks the two other major threats to the environment—pollution and the squandering of living and nonliving resources. Rich nations gobble up more of the world's resources than poor ones and create more wastes. The 1.2 billion people living in prosperity consume 70 percent of the resources. The other 4.8 billion people make do with the remaining 30 percent.

Consider this: the United States, with only 5 percent of the world's population, uses up 25 percent of global resources. Its *ecological footprint* is larger than any other nation's. An ecological footprint is a measure of how much of the Earth's resources are needed to support a lifestyle and absorb the resulting waste products. Footprints vary from country to country. Within a particular country, they differ from individual to individual. Australia and Canada create footprints almost as big as the United States.

The choice of food, transportation, housing, type and amounts of energy usage, and refuse disposal are some of the factors that determine a footprint. For example, someone who drives to work in a gas-guzzling vehicle leaves a bigger footprint than someone who walks or bikes. If every person on the planet lived like a typical American, we would need the materials from four Earths to sustain them.

Human beings compete for resources not only with each other but with other living things, too. The more resources our species use up, the less there is for other kinds of life on Earth. One of the greatest challenges facing humankind is to

The roots of mangrove trees create a sanctuary for young fish, shrimps, and crabs.

83

achieve a sustainable balance between the needs of escalating human populations and the needs of natural ecosystems.

YOUR GENERATION CAN MAKE A DIFFERENCE

The current generation of scientists and policy-makers has had limited success in reversing the decline of the oceans. Your generation will be better equipped to succeed. You and your peers probably have a greater sense of Earth's fragility than your parents and grandparents had when they were young. Too many people in the previous generations were raised with the idea that the ocean's bounty was limitless and that pollution would not cause long-term harm.

Perhaps you will be among the leaders in science or government who will galvanize the effort to restore the health of the ocean and protect its biodiversity. There is much to do. One of the biggest challenges is to find a way to reduce the size and frequency of dead zones. Part of the solution will be to control polluted runoff from farms, streets, and lawns. Maybe you can work to develop effective laws that protect threatened streams, rivers, and coastlines.

Are you up to tackling the problem of global warming? You won't necessarily have to do it alone, as most scientific advances today result from team effort. Advanced technology is needed to make power-generating plants cleaner and more efficient. Will you or your team find an environment-friendly way to soak up excess carbon dioxide emissions from these industrial plants? Do you have a solution for putting out fires in underground coal deposits? Is it possible to make the capture of solar energy more efficient?

New research initiatives are also needed to reduce or eliminate harmful chemicals released by factories into waterways. This could involve the invention of new materials that create less pollution during the manufacturing process and can be readily recycled. Think about all the packaging for food and other materials that your family throws out each week. Can you find a more efficient method to distribute food and other consumer goods? Will you be one of the inventors who discovers new uses for recycled materials? Will you find a better way to manage the disposal of hazardous wastes?

Do you want to protect marine creatures and their habitats near shore?

Perhaps someday you can participate in the ongoing research to control the spread of alien species, such as the European green crab and aggressive Asian clam. Even if these animals are brought under control, much needs to be done to prevent new invaders from taking hold.

The laws protecting marine ecosystems need to be updated. However, before they can be completely overhauled, a better understanding is needed of the dynamics within each kind of ecosystem. Scientists have already begun this research. The results of their studies will someday be used to restore damaged coastal habitats. Maybe in the future you can enhance the work of these scientists.

Perhaps you can work to establish no fish zones in waters surrounding the remaining mangrove swamps, salt marshes, and other nursery habitats for marine organisms. Or you can become involved in land use planning and find a way to protect wetlands bordering the sea, without stifling economic growth in coastal communities.

Another way you could help is to participate in a seafood watch group that monitors the status of fish sold commercially and issues alerts to restaurants and consumers. If you speak another language besides English and have good communication skills, you might be able to influence consumers in a different country.

Are you concerned about bycatch and like to invent new things? Maybe you can devise a better fishing net. If none of these ideas appeals to you there are countless additional projects to be undertaken to improve the conditions of the ocean. If you are a citizen of the United States or Canada, you will be eligible to vote when you turn eighteen. Prepare yourself now by following the news and learning about the issues. Identify which politicians best represent the ideas that you have for making the world a better place. Mark your eighteenth birthday by registering to vote. Then vote your conscience every election day. But you don't have to wait until you're eighteen to make a difference.

What You Can Do Now to Save the Ocean

Today overfishing, pollution, coastal development, global warming, and overpopulation all threaten the sea and the life within it. You may think that as one individual there is little you can do to implement change. However, choices you make now and in the future can help to stop the destruction. When combined with the actions of many like-minded people, the result could be significant.

To help fish stocks recover:

- Make meal choices that will help the recovery of overfished oceanic fish and shellfish species. Until their fisheries recover, avoid eating cod, swordfish, haddock, pollack, snapper, orange roughies, groupers, shark, monkfish, bluefin tuna, and Alaskan king crabs.
- Two or three times a week substitute a vegetarian meal for one that includes meat. (Collectively this action will reduce nutrient pollution from farms.)
- Use phosphate-free laundry detergents. If you use an automatic dishwasher, use a dish-washing detergent with a low phosphate content. Or switch to washing dishes by hand. Dish-washing liquids for the handwashing of dishes are phosphate-free. But they produce too many bubbles to be used in dishwashers. (Collectively these actions will reduce phosphorous pollution.)
- Don't litter—dispose of your trash responsibly, so it doesn't wind up in the ocean.

To curb global warming:

- Reduce your contribution to carbon dioxide emissions by walking, biking, carpooling, or taking public transportation. Buy locally grown food to cut down on the distance your food travels.
- At home, turn on a fan instead of an air conditioner when feasible.
- To save energy, turn off lights, televisions, and CD players when you leave a room.
- Look for energy-efficiency ratings when you or your family buy appliances and electronic equipment. Get the most energy-efficient models that you can afford.
- Plant a tree.

Reduce, reuse, and recycle materials at home and at school to cut down on the amount of new materials that would be used to replace them. Buy recycled products.

Glossary

Algae—simple plantlike organisms containing chlorophyll but lacking roots, stems, and leaves

Algae bloom—the sudden massive growth of algae

Atmosphere—a mixture of gases that surrounds the Earth

Brackish water—water that is somewhat salty. It occurs where freshwater from a river mixes with saltwater from the ocean.

Carbon cycle—the movement of carbon through living and nonliving materials in the environment

Carbon dioxide—an invisible odorless gas consisting of one carbon atom and two oxygen atoms

Carbonic acid—a weak acid formed by dissolving carbon dioxide in water

Climate: the pattern of weather conditions for a particular region over a long period of time

Dead zone—a region of seawater so depleted of oxygen that fish and other sea animals cannot survive in it

Decomposers—organisms that break down large chemicals from wastes or dead organisms into small chemicals

Diatoms—tiny one-celled algae enclosed by a glass shell

Dinoflagellates—types of one-celled algae. Some kinds of dinoflagellates can produce powerful toxins.

Ecologically extinct—a distinct kind of animal or other organism that has been reduced so much in number that it no longer influences its ecosystem

Ecosystem—all the living and nonliving things that interact in a specific area

Estuary—an inlet, lagoon, or bay near the mouth of a river where freshwater and seawater mix

Extinction—the death of all members of a species

Food Chain—the transfer of food energy from one organism to another through predation

Fossil fuels—carbon-rich fuels such as coal, oil, and natural gas, which formed underground from the remains of living things over the course of hundreds of thousands of years

Glacier—a thick mass of ice that doesn't melt in summer. Propelled by gravity, glaciers flow slowly over land.

Global warming—the gradual increase in the average world temperature

Greenhouse effect—the trapping of heat by gases in the atmosphere

Greenhouse gases—carbon dioxide, water vapor, methane, and other gases in the atmosphere that can absorb heat

Habitat—the place where a plant, animal, or other organism lives

Ice age—periods of time lasting tens of thousands of years when much of Europe and North America were covered by glaciers

Invasive species—an organism that is transported to a new environment, where it establishes itself and disrupts the existing ecosystem

Overfishing—the harvesting of a fish species at a rate faster than the species can reproduce and maintain its population size

Permafrost—the permanently frozen soil in the tundra regions near the North and South Poles

Photosynthesis—the process by which plants and plantlike organisms use light energy, carbon dioxide, and water to make sugar and release oxygen

Pollutant—a harmful substance released into the air, soil, or water

Pollution—any change in the environment that has a negative impact on living things

Population—all the members of the same species living in an ecosystem

Red tide—a toxic algae bloom

Respiration—the process by which oxygen combines with simple sugar molecules to release the energy they contain

Sea level—the height of the ocean

Species—a distinct kind of individual plant, animal, or other organism

Toxins—poisonous chemicals that can harm or kill animals and other organisms

Water vapor—the gaseous form of water

Weather—the condition of the atmosphere at a particular place and time

Wetlands—marshes, bogs, and swamps

Further Reading

Books

Bilger, Burkhard. *Earth at Risk: Global Warming.* New York: Chelsea House Publishers, 1992.

Carr, Terry. *Spill! The Story of the Exxon Valdez.* New York: Franklin Watts, 1991.

Collins, Elizabeth. *Earth at Risk: The Living Ocean.* New York: Chelsea House Publishers, 1994.

Dolan, Edward F. *Our Poisoned Waters.* New York: Cobblehill Books, 1997.

Kurlansky, Mark. *The Cod's Tale.* New York: G.P. Putnam's Sons, 2001.

Miller, Christina G., and Louise A. Berry. *Air Alert: Rescuing the Earth's Atmosphere.* New York: Atheneum Books for Young Readers, 1996.

Pringle, Laurence. *Global Warming: The Threat of Earth's Changing Climate.* New York: SeaStar Books, 2001.

Stefoff, Rebecca. *Earth at Risk: Overpopulation.* New York: Chelsea House Publishers, 1993.

Web Sites

"Biodiversity: It Takes All Kinds to Make a World" is a Web site sponsored by the American Museum of Natural History.
http://www.amnh.org/nationalcenter/it_takes_all_kinds/

"Coal Fires"
http://www.gi.alaska.edu/~prakash/coalfires/introduction.html

"The Day the Cats of Minamata, Japan, Threw Themselves into the Bay," a true story by Sandra L. Justus
http://www.geocities.com/AlphaGammaMu_ptk/Minamata.html

Ecovoyagers, Web site provides information on ecological footprints and tips on how to reduce your own.
http://www.ecovoyagers.com/

"The Jubilee Phenomenon" at Auburn University Marine Extension & Research Center
http://www.aces.edu/department/extcomm/publications/anr/anr-834/pdf/anr-834.pdf

"Legacy of an Oil Spill 10 Years after *Exxon Valdez*" is a Web site by the Exxon Valdez Oil
Spill Trustee that provides information about the impact of the oil spill and the
recovery of the region.
http://www.oilspill.state.ak.us/index.html

Remembering Pearl Harbor, a Web site for kids sponsored by the National Park Service
http://www.cr.nps.gov/nr/twhp/wwwlps/lessons/18arizona/18arizona.htm

Safeguarding the Oceans, An Environmental Defense Web Site. To choose the most environmen-
tally friendly fish, click on the "Seafood Selector."
http://www.environmentaldefense.org/system/templates/page/focus.cfm?focus=2

To make informed choices about which seafood products to buy or avoid in order to support
sustainable fisheries, click on "Seafood Watch" at the Monterey Bay Aquarium
Web site's home page.
http://www.mbayaq.org/

The U.S. Environmental Protection Agency's global warming Web site for kids
http://www.epa.gov/globalwarming/kids/index.html

Selected Bibliography

BOOKS

Cramer, Deborah. *Great Waters: An Atlantic Passage*. New York: W.W. Norton, 2001.

Duxbury, Alyn C., Alison B. Duxbury, and Keith A. Sverdrup. *An Introduction to the World's Oceans*, 6th edition. New York: McGraw Hill, 2000.

Earle, Sylvia A. *Sea Change: A Message of the Oceans*. New York: Fawcett Columbine, 1995.

Helvarg, David. *Blue Frontier: Saving America's Living Seas*. New York: W.H. Freeman, 2001.

Woodard, Colin. *Ocean's End: Travels Through Endangered Seas*. New York: Basic Books, 2000.

MAGAZINE AND NEWSPAPER ARTICLES

Dold, Catherine, "The Cholera Lesson," *Discover,* February 1999, pp. 71–75.

Fisher, David E., and Marshall Jon Fisher, "The Nitrogen Bomb," *Discover*, April 2001, pp. 50–57.

Franklin, H. Bruce, "The Most Important Fish in the Sea," *Discover*, September 2001, pp. 44–50.

Hodgson, Bryan, "Alaska's Big Spill: Can the Wilderness Heal?" *National Geographic*, January 1990, pp. 5–43.

Jackson, Jeremy B. C., "What Was Natural in the Coastal Oceans?" *Proc. Natl. Acad. Sci. USA*, Vol. 98, Issue 10, May 8, 2001, pp. 5411–5418.

Jackson, Jeremy B. C., Michael X. Kirby et al., "Historical Overfishing and the Recent Collapse of Coastal Ecosystems," *Science*, Volume 293, July 27, 2001, pp. 629–638.

Kunzig, Robert, "Twilight of the Cod," *Discover*, April 1995, pp. 44–58.

Monastersky, Richard, "Good-bye to a Greenhouse Gas," *Science News,* Volume 155, number 25, June 19, 1999, p. 392.

Revkin, Andrew C., "Sunken Fires Menace Land and Climate," *The New York Times*, January 15, 2002, p. 1.

Savage, Neil, "Greenhouse Effect, R.I.P.," *Discover*, August. 2001, pp. 17–18.

Vesilind, Priit J., "Oil and Honor at Pearl Harbor," *National Geographic*, June 2001, pp. 84–99.

WEB SITES

Chepesiuk, Ron, "A Sea of Trouble?" *Bulletin of the Atomic Scientists*, online, September/October 1997, Volume 53, number 5. An article detailing the possible environmental threat posed by the arsenal of chemical weapons that have been disposed at sea

"Climate Change 2001: Impact, Adaptation and Vulnerability," a report assessing the global-warming threat, issued by the United Nations–sponsored Intergovernmental Panel on Climate Change
http://www.ipcc.ch/

The Heat Is Online, a Web site based on the book *The Heat Is On: The Climate Crisis, The Cover-up, The Prescription* by Ross Gelbspan
http://www.heatisonline.org/main.cfm

The Population Reference Bureau
http://www.prb.org/

The Sierra Club's global population and environment Web site
http://www.sierraclub.org/population/

The Sierra Club's global-warming Web site
http://www.sierraclub.org/globalwarming/

The U.S. Environmental Protection Agency Pfiesteria Web site
http://www.epa.gov/owow/estuaries/pfiesteria/

Index

About the Author

Award-winning author Carole Garbuny Vogel loves the ocean and lives 90 minutes from the beach. Her favorite water sport is boogie boarding, which is a lot like surfing but instead of standing up on the board, she lies flat. On beach days when the waves are small, Carole enjoys reading a good book or strolling on the sand looking for shells.

On workdays, Carole Vogel can usually be found "chained" to her computer, wrestling with words. She specializes in high-interest nonfiction topics for young people. Among her many books are *Nature's Fury: Eyewitness Reports of Natural Disasters* (winner of the Boston Authors Club Book of the Year Award), *Legends of Landforms: Native American Lore and the Geology of the Land* (an NCSS/CBC Notable Social Studies Trade Book), and *Shock Waves Through Los Angeles: The Northridge Earthquake* (placed on the Children's Literature Choice List). Carole Vogel is the coauthor of *The Great Yellowstone Fire*, which was named one of the 100 Best Children's Books of the Century by *The Boston Parents' Paper*.

Carole Vogel's books have been chosen for many reading lists, including Outstanding Science Trade Books by the NSTA-CBC, Best Children's Books of the Year by the Children's Book Committee at Bank Street College of Education, and the Science Books & Films' Best Books for Junior High and High School.

A native Pennsylvanian, Carole Vogel grew up in Pittsburgh and graduated from Kenyon College in Gambier, Ohio, with a B.A. in biology. She received an M.A.T. in elementary education from the University of Pittsburgh and taught for five years before becoming a science editor and author. She keeps in touch with her readership by giving author presentations in schools and libraries.

Carole and her husband, Mark, live in Lexington, Massachusetts, where they enjoy frequent visits from their two children, who recently graduated from college. You can learn more about Carole Vogel at her Web site: *http://www.recognitionscience.com/cgv/*